C000143553

A HISTORY OF GOLF

Henry Cotton

A HISTORY OF
GOLF

Louis T. Stanley

WEIDENFELD AND NICOLSON
London

All photographs are
by the author

Contents

I

In the Beginning

THAT shrewd observer of golfing foibles and theories, Sir Walter Simpson, wrote in 1892 that 'the grounds on which golf is played are called links, being the barren, sandy soil from which the sea has retired in recent geological times. In their natural state links are covered with long, rank, benty grass and gorse ... Links are too barren for cultivation; but sheep, rabbits, geese, and professionals pick up a precarious livelihood on them.' In essence Simpson was right. Many of our finest links have been moulded and shaped by natural forces. The process began when the sea receded leaving sandbanks and channels of salt water that slowly dried out. In time these ridges became wind-scarred sand-dunes of marram while the sheltered valleys were carpeted with bent and fescue that in turn attracted colonies of rabbits, the right ingredients to anticipate a links of excellent golfing turf.

Westward Ho was in that category. Its potential was recognized by General Moncrieffe during a stay with Mr Gosset, the vicar of Northam. Looking across that stretch of low-lying common ground known as Northam, or Appledore Burrows, to the famous Pebble Ridge and the shores of Bideford Bay, his verdict was prophetic, 'Providence obviously designed this for a golf links.' It has become a truly great test of skill in the same way that Sandwich with its towering sandhills and spacious fairways is a course for heroes. No two courses are alike, nor are they expected to be. Favourites are inevitable, sometimes too limited, like the preference of that doyen of writers, John Low. In his opinion championships should be played in alternate years at St Andrews and Hoylake and nowhere else. He argued that the outstanding feature of these two courses

ABOVE Clubhouse of the Royal and Ancient Golf Club known by generations of the world's greatest golfers as the guardian of the game's traditions and arbiter of its rules.

BELOW Royal Birkdale is essentially a natural test with rolling sandhills and willow-scrub rough. The setting lends itself to adventurous golf. There is a streak of fierceness about the lay-out: no domestic tabby but a full-grown tiger. One of the finest courses in England.

was that they produced as winners the best golfers of the year. I question whether this John Low's choice would be approved today, but there is no argument about St Andrews. It is one of the world's greatest tests of a player's skill, yet often initial reaction is not always so complimentary, and critics maintain that its reputation has been exaggerated until gradually a fuller appreciation is felt. Analysis shows that the fine shot is rewarded, if not, it is punished. Every shot has to be carefully planned. No one can ignore the subtlety of natural bunkers ranging from yawning caverns to hidden pot-bunkers. Fairways can deny a level stance, while the contours of enormous plateau greens have curving slopes and undulations which put a premium on reading a line and judging pace.

It is a contest of strategy often influenced, if not resolved, by the wind which is the ultimate hazard on the Old Course, particularly when it sweeps from left to right across the fairways of the first, eleventh, sixteenth and seventeenth. Many of the holes command affection and respect. Together they show why Bobby Jones once said that if he had to play his golf on only one course, he would without hesitation have chosen the Old Course. Such sentiments have been echoed by other great golfers. I think of Tom Watson's tribute that appeared in an issue of *Golf World*:

St Andrews is the first course you think of when you think of championship golf. It is the birthplace of the game. Playing there is a very special experience. Winning there would carry very special meaning for me. The course is virtually everything modern architecture is not. All architects should make a pilgrimage to St Andrews. We've taken the concept of target golf way too literally. The first thing that struck me when I played there in 1978, when I was tied for the lead going into the last round and finished in a tie for fourteenth, was the comparative ease of the first and eighteenth holes. Gene Sarazen likes that. He thinks the critical hole should be halfway through the second nine, rather than have everything boil down to the closing hole. Then there are the double greens, the bunkers with their historic names ... it's a remarkable, memorable place.

Watson's comment that St Andrews is 'the birthplace of the game' is true. The earliest mention of golf being played here is in a parchment preserved in the University Library. It is a licence dated 25 January 1552, granted by John Hamilton:

by the mercie of God archbishop of Sanctandros, Primat and Legat natis of the haill realme of Scotland to the inhabitants of the city in return for permission to plant and plenish 'cuniggis' (rabbits) within the north part of their Common Links next adjacent to the water of Eden, covenant within the City to accept the

Carnoustie at the beginning of the century. Primitive equipment but the Barry Burn had still to be crossed seven times.

The Artisan clubhouse at Nairn left a little to be desired.

Sidmouth was a venue for Edwardian fashion as elegant ladies watched the Triumvirate in action.

The Road Hole at St Andrews looks different but the landmarks and the Swilcan Bridge are the same.

community's right inter alia to play at golf, futball, schuting, at all games with all uther maner of pastime, as ever thai pleis, not only where the 'cuniggis' were plenished but in other parts of the links, and in ony tyme cuming.

Golf was clearly played before that date for the Grant was confirmation of rights previously established by usage. An earlier reference to the game in Scotland occurred when James II decreed in 1457 that 'the futball and the golfe be utterly cripit downe and not usit, and at the bowe merkis be mude at ilke proch Kirk a pair of batts and schiting be usit ilk Sunday. And as tuichande the futball and the golfe we ordane it to be punyst be the baronye unlawe.'

A primitive lay-out must have been in existence before the University was founded in 1413. The number of holes varied over the years. The original links at Leith and Blackheath had five holes, later extended to seven like North Berwick and the London Scottish Volunteers on Wimbledon Common. St Andrews settled for twelve, which eventually became twenty-two. The problem was the narrowness of the strip of land available. Being less than forty yards wide, it ruled out separate holes for going out and coming home. Golfers played eleven holes out to the turn by the Eden estuary and returned using the same fairway and greens.

The twenty-two-hole course began near the Martyr's Monument. In 1764 the Royal and Ancient Club passed a resolution that the first four holes should be converted into two, a change that reduced the round to eighteen. Eventually six of the nine greens were extended laterally to allow two holes to be cut upon them, making possible the enormous double greens for which the Old Course is famous. A new site for the seventeenth green was chosen. When the eighteen separate holes were first played, the original nine holes were used on the outward half and the six holes on the extended greens with the new seventeenth green on the return journey.

By 1842 the general lay-out of the links was as today. The outline of the course has not changed. Up to the First World War there were right-hand and left-hand courses used alternately a week at a time. By accident the 1886 Amateur Championship, won by Horace Hutchinson, was played on the left-hand course. According to the rota, the right-hand one should have been used. The Championship was under way before the officials realized what had happened, the left-hand course being used for the first and last time. Steeped in history and tradition, the old course is a priceless possession, the ultimate test of golf, a centuries-old shrine of golf.

2

Experiments with Club and Ball

SO MUCH for the evolution of the golf links. When it comes to the equipment for playing, it is possible to be even more specific. An Essex artist, Joseph Strutt, collected a considerable amount of material in the last half of the eighteenth century, and from this source he described the various sports and pastimes then popular in England. His comments included:

There are many games played with the ball that require the assistance of a club or bat, and probably the most ancient among them is the pastime now distinguished by the name of Goff. In the northern part of the kingdom, Goff is much practiced. It requires much room to perform this game with propriety, and therefore, I presume it is rarely seen in the vicinity of the metropolis. It answers to a rustic pastime of the Romans, which they played with a ball of leather stuffed with feathers, called *Paganica*, and the goff-ball is composed of the same materials to this day. In the reign of Edward the Third the Latin name *Cambuca* has applied to this pastime, and it derived the denomination, no doubt, from the crooked bat or ball with which it is played.

The identity of the man who fashioned the first golf club remains unknown. Some suggest an evolutionary process and pin-point the *cambuca*, the crooked club or staff used for bandy ball between 1327 and 1377, as its immediate ancestor. I suppose the theory is just possible for we know that a century after the last date golf was being played. More interesting is trying to trace the origin of the game by possible derivations of technical terms. There is the suggestion that *golf* might be a derivation from the German *kolbe*, meaning a club, the Dutch *kolf*, the French *chole*, or the Gothic *kulban*. Probably there is an etymological link, but whether this relationship only indicates types of club games is not clear.

Andrew Lang, for instance, after explaining in a court how kolf was played, summed up: 'clearly kolf is no more kolf than cricket is poker.' Another school of thought argues that the theory of the Dutch origin of Scottish golf cannot be supported by the existence of a common nomenclature. If this theory were true then it would be reasonable to expect that there would be common technical expressions on account of the close relationship between Dutch and old Scotch. But this is not the case.

Attempts have been made to prove that Holland was the native home of golf. *Tee* is said to be derived from *tuitje*, pronounced *toytee* – the heap of sand made by the player with his hand on which the ball was balanced before striking off. On the other hand, *tee* is a good old Scottish word associated with the game of curling. It is also odd that in the search for a suitable word, recourse had to be made to the latter part of the Dutch word, which is only a diminutive, whilst the essential first part was ignored. Not only that, but it should be remembered that the *tee* is *not* the mark, but the place from which the first stroke is played. The 1754 Code of Laws says that 'your tee must be upon the ground', which might be interpreted to mean that no artificial raising of the ball was permitted. Even now *tee* is used to mean *teeing-ground* in the Rules.

Regarding the contents of the golf bag, Sir Walter Simpson is succinct in describing a set of clubs 'as that assortment which the player's caddy carries in a cover on wet days ... On fine days the player carried one club himself, either that he had just used or the one he was about to employ.' Many of these early clubs are now finding their way into leading auction houses, usually fetching incredibly high prices. Many can be seen in the Royal and Ancient Golf Club Museum, useful weapons for coping with Old Course whins. An unusual club found in Holland by Andrew Lang is particularly noticeable. It is a massive lump of iron serving as a head, shaped as a spoon one way, and a driver or putter the other. If weight is a significant factor in a drive, this weapon would be the answer, yet the longest drive ever made with it was roughly 100 yards.

Products of Craftsmen

Many of the other clubs are equally unbalanced, eccentrically shaped with heavy heads, shafts at least 45 inches long, clubfaces with an average length of $4\frac{1}{2}$ inches and $1\frac{3}{4}$ inches in breadth. Thick sheepskin grips measure 3 inches in circumference. In time these crude clubs were replaced by ones

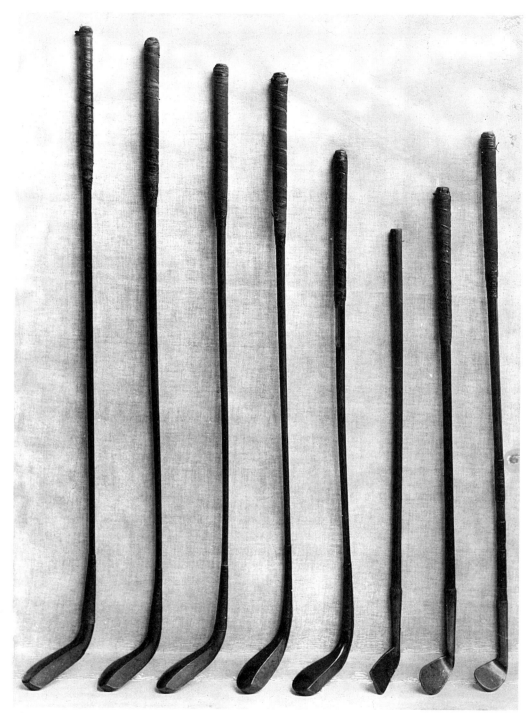

Clubs with a pedigree. From left to right: Driver by William Dunn the Elder (1800–1850); Brassie by McEwen (earliest type) 1850; Long Spoon by Hugh Philp (1800–1856); Short Spoon by McEwen 1850; Putter by Hugh Philp. (From the collection of Whyte Melville. Leslie Balfour Melville won the 1895 Amateur Championship with it.) Earliest type of Sand Iron, 1800.

elegantly crafted in beech, apple, pear and other indigenous hardwoods. Among the craftsmen were James Pett, who made clubs and balls for the Marquis of Montrose in 1672; Robert Wilson of North Street, St Andrews; Henry Mill, supplier of clubs to St Andrews University at the beginning of the eighteenth century; Tom Stewart in Argyle Street and Condie of Market Street in the same town; David Dick of College Wynd, who died in 1731; White, the first blacksmith to concentrate on cleek-making from premises near the Cathedral Pends; James Wilson, one of Hugh Philp's men, who opened his own premises in 1845 on a site now occupied by Rusacks Hotel; but, apart from the McEwans of Musselburgh, none could equal the quality of Hugh Philp's work. This one-time joiner and house painter was appointed clubmaker to the Society of Golfers of St Andrews in September 1819 and moved his works from Argyle Street to a shop by the Union Parlour that served as clubrooms for their members, later transferring to the house that eventually became Tom Morris's shop. On his death in 1856, Phelp was succeeded by Robert Forgan.

The clubs that Phelp made were much lighter in weight than the earlier weapons. Using first-class wood, he gave to all his clubs an unmistakable brilliant finish, the envy of collectors. J. E. Laidlay was particularly fortunate. He was given a complete set by Sir Hew Dalrymple. At auction such a set would realize a world-record price. Even individual Phelp clubs reach over a thousand pounds. Inevitably the field is open for forgeries. Occasionally one appears made of persimmon. That in itself proves it is wrong for this particular wood only appeared in this country from America some fifty years after Phelp's death. Generally speaking the old-type clubs offer a wide range. It is a mistake to imagine that the players of last century had only a few primitive clubs. The opposite is the case, in fact – a ruling by the Royal and Ancient that full complement should be limited to fourteen clubs would have been welcomed. A nineteenth-century set would have included such clubs as the *driver* or *play-club*. The usual length was 45 inches. Robert Chambers described its use: 'The Play-Club is for driving, or, as it is sometimes called, swiping off the tee, and is further used throughout the green if the ball is lying fair, and the distance either a full drive or upwards from the hole to be approached.' Sir Walter Simpson's description in lighter vein reflects a dated sense of humour that must have appealed to some. He refers to the play-club as an

instrument of many parts. It has no legs, but a shaft instead. It has, however, a toe. Its toe is at the end of its face, close to its nose, which is not on its face.

Although it has no body, it has a sole. It has a neck, a head, and clubs also have horns. They always have a whipping, but this has nothing to do directly with striking the ball. There is little expression on the face of the club. It is usually wooden, sometimes, however, it has a leather face. Clubs, without being clothed, occasionally have lead buttons, but never any buttonholes. Club heads are some black, some yellow, but colour is not due to any racial difference. From this description, it will be easy to understand, without a diagram, what the club is like!

The *grassed driver* was regarded as an ordinary play-club with the face set back a little or *spooned* in order to give elevation to the ball when struck. According to Horace Hutchinson the club was a refinement, 'it was only the golfer who was very determined to have no gap in his armour that would carry it.' The third wooden club was the *long spoon*. Not quite so long in the shaft, the face was well 'spooned' or filed to give it even sharper elevation. It was particularly useful when the wind was behind or when the ball was trapped in long grass. The *middle spoon* was similar, shorter with a stiffer shaft. The *short spoon* was even shorter in shaft. According to Robert Chambers, it was frequently in the golfer's hands during the course of the day. It was used for playing bad-lying balls 100 yards or so from the hole in what is termed the 'quarter-game', an asset to the short-game player. The *baffing spoon* was shorter still and very much spooned. It was effective when the ball was about fifty yards from the hole with a bunker intervening. James Balfour left a description: 'To baff a ball is to touch the turf below the ball pretty firmly when it is struck and the ball is thus raised into the air.' Expert performers with the baffy were Sir David Baird, Captain Dalgleish and Sir Robert Hay, all famous St Andrews characters.

The *wooden niblick* had a shaft similar to the driver. It was well 'spooned' and very short with a broad head. It is probable that its inventor played over a course scarred by cart-ruts and sheep-tracks and found the ball could be extracted much easier from these traps if the wooden clubheads were smaller. The result was a club that fitted an ordinary sheep-track. Constant use damaged the sole of the club as it made contact with the stones. A strip of brass screwed on the sole became known as the *brassy*. The *baffy* was made obsolete by the *lofting iron* introduced by Young Tom Morris. The value of excessive length in clubheads was questioned. It was argued that driver-heads should be shorter with the weight centred behind the point on which the ball was struck. It proved an important stage in the design evolution of the golf club. The modification led to the round-faced club known as the *bulger*. Critics questioned whether a ball could be driven straight with convex-shaped clubs. Credit for inventing this club was claimed by Henry Lamb, but Willie Park junior held different views. He stated that 'in 1884 the idea occurred to me of trying a club with a convex instead of the usual straight face. Having made such a club, I played with it that year and the Open Championship of 1885.' His own descriptions of the principle behind the club are interesting: 'In playing with straight-faced clubs it is found that if the ball is struck with the heel of the club it will fly, not in a straight line, but curving towards the right of the player; while if struck with the toe of the club it will curve towards the left. The convex face of the bulger is intended to counteract the effect of hitting off the heel or toe, and ensure straight flight.' Many golfers became converted to the theory of bulger face convexity only to find it failed in practice. The clubface was convex at first, but a few lusty drives quickly hammered it back to level. One caustic critic was Professor Guthrie Tait, father of the well-known Freddie, who dismissed the claims in sarcastic verses under a nom de plume.

There are now nine clubs in the nineteenth-century bag. The next choice is the *putter*. An early writer referred to this club as a 'short-shafted, stiff club, with a large flattish head, and square face; it is used when the ball arrives in close proximity to the hole, generally within twenty yards, with no intervening hazards, and considered the best club for holing-out the ball.' He had conservative tastes, disliking those with double faces, others like swans with curled necks, or shaped like a mallet, and so on. Next is the *driving putter*. James Balfour, writing in 1887, declared that 'the driving putter is never now played with. It was a club with a putter head, but with a flatter angle than a putter, a shaft about the length of a middle spoon, and though stiff, had a spring in it. It was used to play out of bents and thick grass, but as these have now disappeared, so has the club. It was convenient, too, for playing against the wind.'

The complement of wooden clubs is now complete. First of the iron clubs was the *iron putter*, serving as an alternative choice to the wooden putter which it resembled in stiffness. Horace Hutchinson declared that the latter had the wisdom of ages in its favour, but the former was the better weapon for putts up to twenty yards. He felt the wooden putter was safer for the long putt. The next club was the *cleek*, generally regarded as the longest driver of the iron family. Douglas Rolland and John Ball could drive with a cleek as far as a driver. The principle behind its design was to mass the weight behind the point of impact with the ball, without upsetting its balance. It was also used for holing-out when the greens were fast or the ball 'cupped'. A useful utility iron.

Now a variety of irons. The *driving iron* was used for long distances when height was needed. The *medium* or ordinary iron was for shorter distances. It lofted the ball and was ideal for 'half' shots. The *lofting iron* was for 'short approach shots'. A. F. Macfie, the first Amateur Champion, regarded it as a favourite club. Willie Park attempted to improve its use by introducing *Park's Patent Lofter*. Its shape brought the top part of the blade nearer the ball, less turf was taken and more loft given. The blade was concave giving additional backspin to the ball and was claimed to raise a half-topped ball more effectively.

Three more iron clubs and the bag is more or less complete. The *iron niblick* was for bunker-play or when trapped in a cart-rut. Heavily made with a short round head, it went through the sand easier than a heavy iron. The *President* was a niblick with a hole through its head. It had a drawback, a tendency to strike the ball twice with the club, thus losing the hole by penalty. Finally, the club that was a compromise between a niblick and the lofting iron – the *mashie*.

The full bag came to nineteen clubs:

Wooden Clubs	driver, or play-club
	grassed driver
	long spoon
	middle spoon
	short spoon
	baffing spoon
	niblick
	brassy
	bulger
	putter
	driving putter
Iron Clubs	iron putter
	cleek
	driving iron
	medium, or ordinary iron
	lofting iron
	niblick
	president
	mashie

The range was extensive, but the clubs were clumsy and lacked balance. Many had a touch of individuality. This was shown when Tom Kidd, one of the longest driving professionals of his day, became the owner of an exceptionally fine driver made by Old Tom Morris, with a long shaft, finely shaped, and thick at the leather; head long and narrow, and face reasonably deep. As the years passed the light beechwood mellowed into a rich amber shade. When Kidd died, the club passed to an English golfer. It stayed in a club locker for nine years before it found another owner, who took it to St Andrews on a golfing holiday. On the first tee he was asked by Tom Morris how the club had come into his possession. Despite its altered appearance, the club was recognizable. Unlike today's weapons, it had individuality.

Matched sets of clubs were to follow, but John Low anticipated the development at the beginning of this century. In *Concerning Golf*, he deplored the difficulty of finding good irons and made these suggestions for an answer: 'The answer is simple. Nearly every golfer has one good iron, possibly a driving mashie. Take it to a local club-maker, or one of the St Andrews makers. Order three clubs exactly the same shape and lie; the ordinary driving mashie, the same club with three greater grades of loft, viz, a set of irons, same weight and lie, same balance, same class of shaft, and same thickness of grip.' Such was the foundation of the sophisticated clubs of today, unrecognizable in material, but the principle the same. There are always freak clubs that strive to receive official blessing. Nothing new. There is the temptation of over-corrugated, ribbed, or slotted clubfaces, as when Jock Hutchinson won the Open Championship aided by phenomenal pitching. His irons had been so fiercely punched that every pitch stopped dead on the St Andrews greens. At that time the ploy was legitimate. Then Fairlie introduced a swan-necked club with the face brought forward beyond the line of the shaft. In 1904 the Schenectady putter virtually won the British Amateur title for Walter Travis, but was later made illegal. In the hickory days experiments were made with different woods for shafts. Lancewood, lemonwood, blue-mahoo, green-heart, orangewood, even malacca canes by Gilbert Mitchell-Innes, until hickory was accepted as the best.

Those days have gone, but the clubs have become collectable, often fetching high prices at auction. Brown's 1910 patent *Rake* iron by Winton of Montrose realized £4,000; a Robertson long-nosed fruitwood-head hickory-shafted driver, dated about 1855, fetched £2,500; even earlier but of interest to a golfing historian was a *Pall Mall-Jeu de Mail* hardwood iron bound club, French eighteenth century, worth £12,000; a *Dutch Kolf club*, early nineteenth century with an iron-faced brass head was sold for £2,000; an unusual golf clubhead, *c.* 1600–1650, of lead and tin, impressed with three crosses for the City Arms of Amsterdam, found a buyer for £8,000. It is possible to find many old clubs of interest in junk shops, like a *rut iron* by John Gray dated about 1850, for a couple of pounds. Others that have been unearthed in dusty corners include a long-nosed putter by Robert Forgan, a bulger driver by William Hunter, and a Schenectady aluminium putter. Would-be collectors should be on the look-out for any club stamped T. Morris, particularly bulbous-headed putters; McEwan's beautiful wooden clubs; J. H. Taylor's wooden putters; other famous names like Willie Park, Auchterlonie, J. Anderson, Willie Dunn and Harry Vardon. The range of collectable clubs include baffing spoons, wry-necked iron putters, smooth-faced irons, brass-soled wooden niblicks, jiggers, early cleeks, and mallet-headed putters. Freak clubs occasionally turn up, like four in a lot at a Sotheby sale that had a wooden brass-soled croquet-type three-sided putter, a T-shaped putter, an aluminium circular putter and a hammer-shaped club. They were not only of unusual interest, but a sound investment.

Development of the Golf Ball

Old golf balls are just as collectable with prices at times equally high. Dating is easier as the various stages of evolution can be authenticated. Much of the early history centres round the Robertson family with emphasis on Allan Robertson, the first professional golfer of any consequence. Contemporary pen portraits at times err on the side of exaggeration, like that of the Reverend J. G. McPherson who described Allan as the greatest golfer of all time in his book *Golf and Golfers Past and Present* written in 1891 from a country manse. More restrained was the description by James Balfour in a shilling paper-clad book entitled *Reminiscences of Golf on St. Andrews Links* in 1887. A copy was sold at auction in London quite recently for £2,000. Leslie Balfour-Melville was the son of this golfer, a Medallist of the Royal and Ancient, whose description was more authentic:

Allan Robertson and his father and grandfather had been ball-makers, when feather balls were the only balls, for more than a hundred years. He was a short, little, active man, with a pleasant face, small features, and a merry twinkle in his eye. He was universally popular, not a bit forward, but withal easy and full of self-respect. He generally wore a red, round jacket, and played constantly with gentlemen, both in matches of great importance, and in those that were only more or less important. His style was neat and effective. He held his clubs near the end of the handle, even his putter high up. His clubs were light, and his stroke an easy, swift switch. With him the game was one as much of head as of hand. He always kept cool and generally pulled through a match even when he was behind. He was a natural gentleman, honourable and true. He died of jaundice on 1st September 1859, when only about the age of forty-four, much regretted.

Earlier sources confirm the Robertson family reputation as golf ball makers. Mathieson's poem *The Goff*, published in 1743, a copy of which was sold at auction in 1985 for a five-figure sum, anticipates a match:

> Two balls with careful eye,
> That with *Clarinda*'s breasts for colour vye,
> The work of *Bobson* who, with matchless art,
> Shapes the firm hide, connecting every part,
> Then in a socket sets the well-stitch'd void
> And thro' the eyelet drives the downy tide;
> The feathers harden and the leather swells;
> He crams and sweats, yet crams and urges more
> Till scarce the turgid globe contains its store ...
>   Soon as *Hyperion* gilds old *Andrea*'s spires
> From bed the artist to his cell retires;
> With bended back, there plies his steely awls,
> And shapes and stuffs and finishes the balls.

It is accepted that Bobson who lived by Andrea's spires was a Robertson who lived at St Andrews. A century later the Robertson skill as a ball-maker was confirmed by George Fullerton Carnegie, an Angus laird, born at Pitarrow in 1800, who published a poem *Golfiana* in 1833 for private circulation in which he described St Andrews and contemporary characters. Peter Robertson died in 1803. His son, David, is referred to in Carnegie's poem:

> Great Davie Robertson, the eldest cad,
> In whom the good was stronger than the bad;
> He sleeps in death! and with him sleeps a skill
> Which Davie, statesmanlike, would wield at will!
> Sound be his slumbers! yet if he should wake
> In worlds where golf is play'd, himself he'd stake
> And look about and tell each young beginner,
> 'I'll gie hald-ane – nae mair, as I'm a sinner.'

> He leaves a son, and Allan is his name,
> In golfing far beyond his father's fame.

David Robertson was noted as a player and teacher, but his status was that of a senior caddie, 'the oldest of the cads'. The term professional was then unknown. Davie was the last of the senior caddies; Allan was the first of the professionals, with an established reputation as a ball-maker.

Allan Robertson, Pioneer of Golf Ball Evolution

In practical terms, the method of making golf balls was uniform up to 1848. Robertson was assisted by Tom Morris and Lang Willie. These three worked in Allan's kitchen, the finished balls being sold through a window at the back of the house by the corner of Links and Golf Place. The manufacturing processes were lengthy and tedious. The balls were made of strong leather cases stuffed with boiled feathers. The leather had to be cut into three strips, softened by an application of water and alum to enable it to be sewn together with waxed thread, the feathers being rammed by a stout stuffing-iron through a small hole left in the cover. After being sewn up, the ball, which was frequently more oblong than round, received three coats of paint. They were never really satisfactory and took too long to make. A skilled workman could only average about three or four a day, and the seams were always weak. In dry weather there was the danger of them being cut open by the club, whilst under wet conditions the ball invariably burst, and caddies, forewarned, armed themselves with ample reserves before setting out. Moreover the cost was high, a factor largely responsible for the relatively small number of golfers at this period.

Then in 1848 the rumour spread of a new golf ball, not only cheaper but which lasted much longer than the feathered variety. The gutta-percha ball had arrived. It came about almost by chance. The Reverend James Paterson, a missionary in India, sent to his home in St Andrews a black marble idol which he intended to donate to the college museum. To protect it from damage on the long voyage, the idol was packed in a crate with strips of gutta-percha for additional protection. Instead of throwing them away, the Paterson brothers tried their hands at moulding golf balls. To their surprise the roughly shaped objects flew better than the balls then in use. The method they employed was described to me by Willie Auchterlonie, who won the Open in 1893. The balls were made by hand

Allan Robertson, short and stocky, immensely proud of the fact that he had never been beaten.

out of sheet gutta-percha. This was cut into pieces, softened in hot water, drawn out in the form of a ribbon, wound up into a ball and pressed with the hand on a smooth board. It was then heated again and pressed until it was as solid as possible, the ball being rounded in the hands, as moulds were then unknown. Finally, they were dropped into cold water to harden and kept continually moving about to keep them round, because whenever they became still in the water that part which came above the surface tended to lose its shape.

There was one serious fault about those early balls. However carefully they were made, when first used they ducked violently in flight, but after receiving cuts and hacks through rough usage by cleeks, the trouble was not so noticeable. They flew better at the end of the day. The erratic behaviour was due to the hand-rolling method on a flat board. It was solved by hammering with the chisel end of the clubmaker's hammer a series of small lines set close together. One of the first to adopt this method was a St Andrews saddler in South Street, but it was a slow tedious business. Marking by moulds had yet to be adopted.

The ball-makers were alarmed by the introduction of the gutta-percha ball for the leather trade was the only one the town possessed, orders coming from all parts of the country and the colonies. This can be seen by the records in Robertson's shop. In 1840 the output was 1,021 balls; in 1841 the total was 1,392; in 1844 the figure rose to 2,456. More disturbing was the fact that anyone could mould a gutta-percha ball after a little experience. The demand for skilled craftsmen would cease. Robertson and Morris swore never to touch them. It is recorded that Robertson used to buy all the gutta-percha balls found in the whins and try to burn them. Unfortunately Morris took part in a friendly match in which these balls were used. Robertson was so annoyed, he ended their partnership. Morris opened a shop of his own where he made both kinds of balls as well as clubs. Not long afterwards Robertson had second thoughts. Instead of bribing caddies to give him all the gutties they could find so he could burn them, he realized the new ball need not ruin his trade. Gourlay had been just as fearful. He went to Musselburgh and watched Admiral Maitland Dougall using a guttie and had been astonished to see how the ball flew, and, being round, rolled straight to the hole on the putting green. Sharing Robertson's alarm, and having an order from Sir David Baird to send him some feather balls whenever he had a supply, Gourley forwarded to him that evening six dozen. Not surprising Sir David was one of the last to use featheries until his stock ran out.

Ball-makers realized that the number of new players would increase having been deterred by the short life of the expensive balls. Robertson also anticipated the need for a new type of iron club. The feathery ball had jumped off the face of a wooden putter, while the rounded shape of the gutta called for a rolling shot instead of the former stroke. A putting cleek was introduced for the greens, revolutionizing the short game with irons and unquestionably influenced the club-making industry. Allan Robertson bridged the gap between the feathery and gutta-percha eras.

Robertson's reputation as a player was somewhat exaggerated, but he was a fine player. He was the first man to break 80 on the Old Course, carding 79 in a match against Bethune of Blebo on 15 September 1858. His card read:

Out: 4-4-4-5-5-6-4-4-4 – 40
In: 4-3-5-6-4-5-5-4-3 – 39 – 79

Robertson also took part in a series of challenge matches, the biggest stake-money clashes of the nineteenth century. In 1849 £400 was waged when Robertson and Tom Morris took on the Dunns of Musselburgh. The match was over three greens – Musselburgh, St Andrews and North Berwick, in that sequence. Musselburgh saw the Dunns victorious by the huge margin of 13 and 12. St Andrews evened the score after a close fight. The Robertson-Morris partnership went on to win the decider and the series by an aggregate of two holes.

Allan Robertson was a landmark in the history of the game. He never held the position of Club Professional, in fact his name is mentioned only twice in the Royal and Ancient Minutes. The first time was in October 1856 when the Green Committee was authorized 'to expend the sum of £25 in placing the putting greens into better order, under the super-intendence of Allan Robertson.' The only other entry was on 28 September 1859 when the following resolution was entered:

That this Meeting have heard with deep regret of the death of Allan Robertson and they desire to record in their Minutes the opinion universally entertained of the almost unrivalled skill with which he played the Game of Golf combining a ready and correct judgment with most accurate execution. They desire also to express their sense of the propriety of his whole conduct and unvarying civility with which he mingled with all classes of Golfers, of his cordiality to those of his own, of his integrity, his happy temper and the anxiety which he always mani-fested to promote the comfort of all who frequented the Links. They desire an extract of this Minute to be transmitted to his widow with an expression of their sympathy in her affliction.

To this might be added as a postscript the words of the Reverend W. W. Tulloch ... 'Allan Robertson was the most outstanding figure and the most interesting personality on any links in the first half of the nineteenth century.'

Experimental Stages

Experiments still continued with ball production. The 'Stewart Patent' ball was an attempt by Commander Stewart to introduce a composition ball filled with steel filings. It had certain good points, but the decisive defect was its weight. Eventually an Edinburgh firm produced the 'Eclipse' ball, which had several features that made it preferable to the gutta-percha. It was softer. It could be compressed by the fingers, but the compression came out again. Clubs were spared the damage caused by the hard gutty. Ill-treatment by an iron did not alter its spherical form. It was a good ball in the wind, ran true on the greens and was generally regarded as the best putting-ball so far produced. Critics argued it had a shorter flight than the gutty, it was almost impossible to make approach shots stop dead, and after a round the paint came off in patches. On balance durability and toughness won. It was rechristened the 'putty' as against the 'gutty'. The professionals were suspicious of its almost indestructible qualities, the only one converted being Willie Fernie, who made the best of both worlds. He would play with a 'putty' going out in a strong wind at St Andrews, taking advantage of a ball that kept low and straight, but reverted on the homeward half to a gutta-percha, finding it easier to make it 'stop' on the greens downwind. Horace Hutchinson won the first two British Amateur Championships with an 'Eclipse', whilst Andy Stewart won three St Andrews medals playing with the same ball on each occasion. Suddenly for some reason the quality of the ball changed. The manufacturers, trying to make them harder, renewed their challenge to the gutta-percha. Before the century ended, the attempt had failed.

Coburn Haskell was next on the scene. The ball he introduced was the result of conversations at the home of Ernest Kirk in Cleveland, Ohio, during the summer of 1898. Both felt the gutta-percha ought to be replaced by an improved ball. Rubber, wound under tension, was a possible answer. Kirk, a leading figure in the American rubber industry, obtained rubber strands from his factory. Both men wound the first ball by hand, covering it with gutta-percha. Their club professional tried it out without knowing anything about the experiment. The first drive was the longest seen on that course. Two years passed before a machine was assembled to do the winding, followed by a period of testing. When launched the Haskell killed the gutta-percha overnight. The market switched to America. By the summer of 1903 American manufacturers had despatched 40,000 dozen Haskells to this country. Thus was introduced the prototype of the modern ball. It contained 190 yards of thread which was stretched to eight times its original length, roughly a mile, then wound round a small piece of wood or tiny bag of gelatine.

Haskell's claim to be the first to introduce the rubber-cored ball has been disputed. Willie Park left it on record that he anticipated the possibility much earlier. He wrote:

... when I was about eleven or twelve years of age I was of an inventive turn of mind, and I remember that I applied myself to the production of a ball that would go farther than the gutties, and indeed, may claim to have been the maker of the first rubber ball. I made a mixture of ground cork, ground rubber and gutta-percha, and forced it down a funnel into an iron mould. The ball that resulted after the mixture had set seemed all right, but after playing a few shots, it expanded enormously, and I had to give the idea up.

Park was born on 4 February 1864 at Musselburgh. The date of his experiment would be either 1875 or 1876. Bernard Sayers likewise pressed his claim. At the time when there were several law-suits about rubber-cored patents, he wrote:

... a great many of my customers always asked for balls that would bounce well, and I remember trying the experiment – and it succeeded well too – of filing down a lot of rubber into small particles, and then, when I was working up the gutta ball, and just before I put it into the mould to press, I rolled it quite full of these rubber filings, which were well mixed up with the gutta. We found that the balls so treated had always more go in them than the plain gutta. This, I venture to think, would be amongst the earliest varieties of the rubber ball.

The first professional to demonstrate the possibilities of the Haskell in a championship was Sandy Herd. He used to say that his success in the 1902 Open at Hoylake was in part due to John Ball. At that time Haskell balls were scarce in this country and Herd was far from being converted. The day before the championship started, he played a practice round with Ball. The professional's driving was up to its usual standard. Even so he could not equal the length of his amateur opponent who was playing with one of the new balls. He was so impressed that Ball let him try one. After a few holes, Herd decided to use them in the championship. Jack Morris provided him with three. History records the result.

3

Continuity with the Past

ONE way of recalling the early days of golf is to trace the history of old golfing trophies. The Gold Medal of the Royal Liverpool Golf Club at Hoylake is an instance. Striking in appearance, it bears the club crest, rose and thistle enamel surround, with the words 'Liverpool Golf Club 1869' inscribed on the edge. The golden crown and 'Royal' were added later. First played for in frightful weather, it was won by John Dun, an eminent club member, with a score of 96, compiled by playing nine holes twice. In those days Hoylake was a sleepy fishing hamlet, and the links by the shore of the Dee estuary vied with a race-course for pride of place. The last race took place on 8 April 1876. Two weather-beaten posts in the middle of a fairway serve as a reminder of days when hoof-marks were common hazards. A landmark that stood out in Hoylake history was the Royal Hotel built in 1792 by Sir John Stanley. Horace Hutchinson left his impressions ... 'there was great fun in the musical evenings in the bar parlour of the Royal Hotel – but bar parlour sounds a little ominous but I never remember seeing a man in it who could not talk straight nor walk straight out of it – and some of the golfers had great voices. Tom Potter, popular member of the Free Foresters' Cricket Club, was honorary secretary and there were names like Pendulum Brown, Alec Sinclair and George Dunlop.' When the Gold Medal was introduced, John Ball was about seven years of age. He eventually won it thirteen times, a remarkable record, but then John Ball was a remarkable man. His partnership with his father was a strong pairing of golfing skills; there was a permanent challenge to play any two. Rarely did they lose.

The Silver Club of St Andrews has a long history. It began with the famous minute of 1754, signed by a dozen subscribers, throwing the competition open to all golfers in Great Britain and Ireland. The organizers went to a great deal of trouble to ensure that the first match would be a success. Specific provisions were laid down. 'Every victor is to append a silver ball to the club for the year he wins. No coaches, chaises or other wheel machines or people on horseback or dogs of any kind are to be admitted on the links when the match for the Silver Club is in progress.' Notices were inserted in both the Edinburgh newspapers a month before the contest. But in spite of the preparations only four golfers met on the first tee on 14 May and the Silver Club was 'gained by Bailie William Landale, merchant of St Andrews, in testimony whereof the hail sub-scribers who player have hereto set their hands.' Signed John Stuart, George Moncrieff, John Whyte-Melville, Wolfe Murray, Sir Hugh Lyon Playfair, George Glennie, Murray Belshes and many others.

The last named is remembered as one of the most tireless workers the Royal and Ancient Club has had. In the Royal and Ancient minutes are copies of letters that passed between Murray Belshes and Sir Herbert Taylor, private secretary to William IV. They explain how His Majesty consented to become Patron of the Club and how the designation of 'Royal and Ancient' came to be bestowed. At the outset the request that the King as Duke of St Andrews would become the Patron was declined as acceptance would encourage similar requests from other Societies and might prove embarrassing; the designation 'Royal and Ancient' was, however, approved.

Belshes expressed gratitude for the latter but regrets about the former. He stated he was unaware of such a ruling. The request had been prompted by the fact that Lord Kinnaird had informed him of the King's consent to become Patron of the Perth Society and had approved the style of 'Royal'. He had assumed that preference, if any, would have been given to the Golf Club of St Andrews seeing that the King was Duke of St Andrews, that the club was almost a century older than Perth, and that the membership of St Andrews was drawn from the nobility and gentry of Scotland, many in different parts of the world. Such persistent arguments gained the point. In a further letter Sir Herbert admitted that the precedent mentioned had been overlooked. His Majesty would therefore grant the wish of the club that he should become its Patron in his capacity as Duke of St Andrews.

Another example is the Silver Cup of the Royal Musselburgh which was presented in 1774 by Thos McMellan. A silver medal inscribed with his name and date show him to be the winner of that year. Members were conscious of the historic value of the trophy. Before 1841 the winner was not allowed to take it out of the town but in that year the rule was repealed. In 1874 it was felt that 'considering the irreparable loss the Club would sustain in the event of any damage occurring to the Club's Silver Cup, in future the Cup remain in the possession of the Club – the same to be deposited in the bank – the winner to be allowed to have the Cup at any time but not for a period exceeding 24 hours, on application to the Secretary, who shall give a delivery order in exchange for a receipt in writing.' I believe the ruling still stands, for when I visited Musselburgh some years ago and asked to see the trophy, I was taken to the local bank for viewing.

There used to be considerable ceremony with the tournament for this cup in the last century. In the morning it was placed in Widow Cochrane's, where local golfers used to foregather, in anticipation of the procession. The town drummer, for a fee of three shillings, would walk in front followed by the club officer carrying the cup with its medals, with members and caddies bringing up the rear as the procession made its way down the High Street to the links. When the event was over, the return journey was made to Widow Cochrane's.

This procedure is similar to the competition for the Silver Club of the Honourable Company. The record books shows that the City of Edinburgh used 'to intimate by Tuck of Drum, through the City, the day upon which it shall be annually played for, and to send the Silver Club to Leith upon the morning appointed for the Match.' The first such competition was won by John Rattray, who must have been an interesting character. He was the son of a bishop and a member of the College of Surgeons. When the Highland Army left Edinburgh on its march south he was compelled to join the Highlanders in the early hours of the morning in order to attend the wounded. Captured at the Battle of Culloden, he was imprisoned in Scotland and later in London but was released in 1747 through Lord President Duncan Forbes, also a member of the Gentlemen Golfers. He died in 1771 but his name does not appear in the minutes after 1759.

The Silver Cross of the Royal Aberdeen Golf Club has had a chequered history. It was given to the club in 1852 in an attempt to persuade their members to practise at certain 'hazardous holes,' including one 'beyond the whins of the Old Town Links' on a new course that had been laid out by Willie Park of Musselburgh. The Silver Cross was played in summer on account of the high tides that flooded the links in winter and made these holes unplayable. The minute book further records that 'it was also ordained that there should be a beefsteak and a tumbler of punch after the competition.' The provision did not appeal as the competition was held only twice, in 1853 and 1854. The following year no members competed for the cross except for the honorary secretary, Arthur Thompson, who suspended the event *sine die*. It was revived in 1868 but about the year 1872 the Silver Cross disappeared and a new cross had to be provided, as the minutes of the general meeting on 4 May 1874 indicate: 'The Captain produced the new Silver Cross made by Messrs Mackay and Cunningham, Edinburgh, in room of the old one, which unaccountably disappeared some time before, and gave it into the custody of the Secretary, to be handed by him to the winner when the ties were played off.'

Five years later we find this further entry concerning a meeting of the Council on 7 April 1879: 'The Secretary reported that the old Silver Cross which had been missing since about the year 1872 had been found by Mrs Simpson (the stewardess) in one of the drawers of the writing case in the Clubhouse and it was resolved that it should be given as a permanent prize to the winner of the Silver Cross at the Spring Meeting.' The winner was G. G. Smith with a score of 167. Twenty-nine years later he restored the trophy to the club. The same club has the Strangers' or, as it was later called, the Midsummer Medal, dating from October 1865. Made of silver, it was intended 'to induce strangers to visit the Links', conditions being that the event should be open to all comers except professionals, the medal to be the property of any player winning three times in succession. The idea failed. No stranger ever won. After a few years it was played for as a club medal.

The history of trophies supplemented by the minutes provides reliable background of a golf club's existence. This is shown in the case of Kingsbarns Golf Club, Fife, which ceased to exist in 1851. By means of trophies and club minutes it is possible to piece together a rough history, although there is doubt about the date of its founding. The first minute is dated 2 May 1835, but the minute for 3 August 1849 infers an earlier origin. One of the medals indicates 1823 and a minute dated 4 September 1793 of the neighbouring Crail Golfing Society, which goes back to 1786, refers to the Kingsbarns Club as follows: 'It is agreed that the members of the Kingsbarns Golfing Society be allowed to appear on the Links at Crail in the uniform belonging to their own Society, Blue Jackets.' The choice of colour was unusual but the Crail fairways must have been a study in contrasts with the home club uniform of scarlet jackets with a plain yellow button blending with the less familiar blue.

On 1 June 1838 we find another medal being ordered. On 2 May 1840 a gold one was presented by bachelor members of the Society. On 5 March 1841 Captain Corstorphine gave a snuff-box richly mounted with silver appendages. On 7 May Captain Feilden presented another medal for competition among members of every Golf Society in Fife. Everything suggests a small but flourishing club. Occasionally there were outside distractions, such as on 5 November 1836 when 'in consequence of the lateness of the harvest none of the members appeared on the golfing ground.' But in 1846 the secretary resigned after thirty-two years in office. By 3 August 1849 it was decided to suspend the operations of the Society, a decision taken with regret for we read: 'In retracing the past none can fail to bear upon their remembrance the many happy meetings that have been held. Only one of its original members has his name remaining on the roll – the chaplain. Many of its members have passed the bourne ... much kindly intercourse has been maintained and not a few deeds of charity done.' In the event of a future revival it was decided that the records and medals be placed in a box and left in the keeping of Captain Corstorphine of Pittourie at Kingsbarns.

> 'When restored then
> *Palmam qui meruit ferat,*
> In the meantime
> *Sic transit gloria mundi*'

It was a gallant way to close the last chapter of a club's history, whose memory would have been erased had it not been for its trophies and minutes.

4

Vintage Years

Harold Hilton

1869 MIGHT be described as a vintage year in amateur golf for it produced some of the greatest of the old school of golfers, players like Sydney Fry, Harry Colt, John Low and J. B. Pease, better known as Lord Wardington. Freddie Tait is usually included on the list, although he was born in Edinburgh on 11 January 1870. It seems fitting, however, that he should be placed in the same year as his rival, Harold Hilton. The latter ranks as one of the finest score players this country has known. The present generation knows of Hilton, if at all, by legend and fact, by photographs, record books, possibly by the amusing way his cap used to fall off as the club came through, but not many can trace his playing career in detail. Very briefly I can detail his golfing record up to the beginning of this century.

Hilton learned his golf at Hoylake. His early life was closely associated with the game. Apart from living close to the links, the day school he attended turned out such golfers as John Ball, the Crowthers, Herbert Tweedie and W. More. Hilton was eight years of age when he made his first competitive appearance. It was the competition at Hoylake for boys under sixteen, who played the full eighteen holes, and for boys under twelve, who had to play only twelve holes. Full of ambition, Hilton entered for the major event and was out of his depth. The next year he entered the junior section and won the first prize from scratch, following it the next season by winning the senior scratch medal. In the spring of 1887 Hilton joined the Royal Liverpool Golf Club, the season that the Amateur

Championship was due to be held at Hoylake. The small entry of thirty-three included for the first time the name of Harold Hilton. He reached the second round, only to be beaten by John Ball, Sen. His next appearance was even shorter-lived: J. E. Laidlay defeated him on the last green in the first round.

The event was held again in Hoylake in 1890. This time Hilton survived three rounds before losing to John Ball on the 16th green. At St Andrews in 1891 Hilton saw the chance of winning his first Amateur Championship snatched away by his rival J. E. Laidlay, who won at the 20th in the final. Hilton made his bow in the Open Championship the same year and finished second amateur to Mure Fergusson. 1892 was his first outstanding season. The Amateur at Sandwich saw him defeat Laidlay, his conqueror of 1889 and 1891, in the first round, and go on to the final, where he was defeated by John Ball at the 17th. After this came Hilton's success at Muirfield in the Open Championship. He was undecided about playing. His parents and employer were opposed, but he decided in favour and journeyed by the night train. There was only time for one day's practice. He crammed in three rounds. The first round proper – 78 – left him four strokes behind the leader, Horace Hutchinson. The second round was 81, eight strokes behind the same leader. 72 for the third round placed him in second place, three strokes behind Ball. In the last round he was left with an 8 to win the championship. Holing-out in 6 settled the issue.

Then began the trying chapter in a successful golfer's career, the time when a reputation has to be upheld. The Amateur Championship at Prestwick brought Freddie Tait and Hilton together for the first time. The Englishman was beaten on the 16th green. The Open Championship was played on the same course. Hilton's first round was disastrous. He was out in 37, but required 51 for the homeward half, largely through a 10 caused by having an argument with a wall. The event was won by Willie Auchterlonie and marked the first appearance of Harry Vardon and J. H. Taylor. The 1894 Amateur at Hoylake saw Hilton again defeated by Tait. The final was fought out by John Ball and Mure Fergusson. After a hard fight, in which Fergusson looked as if he had the measure of Ball, the match went to the Cheshire player.

Hilton failed in the Open of that season, which was won by Taylor at Sandwich, the first amateur, Freddie Tait, being twenty strokes behind. 1895 saw Hilton troubled with a wrist injury. He won his first round in the Amateur at St Andrews against C. E. Dick, but was beaten at the 16th in the next by William Greig. He also shaped badly in the Open at St

ABOVE Elegant clubhouse of the Royal Liverpool Golf Club . . . a proud club with a proud tradition.

BELOW Royal Hotel, Hoylake, former home of John Ball and his more famous son: one-time clubhouse of the Royal Liverpool Golf Club. The hotel was demolished some years ago.

Andrews, where bad luck robbed Sandy Herd of the victory which went to Taylor for the second year in succession. The Amateur at Sandwich in 1896 rewarded Hilton with the easy half of the draw. His round with Colt coincided with a freak storm, and after a gruelling match Hilton won at the 20th. He reached the final, where he met Tait. The latter was on top form and won easily by 8 and 7. The Open at Muirfield was uneventful for Hilton, but it marked the arrival of Vardon.

After three years of indifferent golf Hilton entered the successful season of 1897. Apart from a failure in the Amateur, he won almost every other event, including the Open Championship at Hoylake, the first time it had been played on that course. 1898 saw the Amateur at Hoylake, and another meeting between Hilton and Tait, which ended in an overwhelming victory for the latter, who went on to win the event. The Open was won by Harry Vardon, Hilton finishing two strokes behind Vardon and one behind Park. 1899 produced a memorable championship. Prestwick was the course. Once again Hilton met Tait and the result went in favour of the Scot. The final between Tait and Ball produced a dour fight. Nationalistic feelings ran high. After a close duel, Ball won at the 37th. 1988 saw Vardon add a second title to his belt. The opening year of the century coincided with Hilton gaining what he had struggled to win for twelve years, the title of Amateur Champion. Sandwich was the scene. There were two regrettable gaps. Freddie Tait had passed away. John Ball was still in South Africa. Hilton's victims included Robert Maxwell, then playing strongly and winner of the St George's Vase, and John Graham Robb, who reached the final after beating Bramston. Hilton won decisively by 8 and 7.

Hilton repeated his Amateur success the following year at St Andrews, and again in 1911 and 1913, as well as adding the American Amateur Championship in 1911. He became the first player to capture the world's two leading amateur events in the same year. Hilton's record was outstanding, but equally remarkable was his run of defeats by Freddie Tait, the only golfer whom the Englishman feared.

The Reign of John Ball

Since the Amateur Championship was inaugurated in 1885, only a handful have won the title more than once. Of this small band of men, the finest perhaps was John Ball. His first success came in 1872 when, as a lad of eight years he won the Boys' Medal at Hoylake. Seven years later

John Ball was a remarkable golfer, a legend at Hoylake, a loner on the links with his red-topped stockings, an heroic shot-maker.

he finished only eight strokes behind the winner of the Open Championship. His prowess in the Open changed the outlook of amateur golf, especially after he became the first amateur to win this event. The Amateur Championship was his favourite. He won it on no less than eight occasions. His double victory in both events in 1890 was not equalled until Bobby Jones carried everything before him forty years later. In spite of these and many other victories, John Ball always remained modest, retiring and aloof. Seldom did he talk of his triumphs and avoided any public demonstration after his successes. In this respect it is recorded how, after he had won a championship, the population of the fishing village of Hoylake decided to give him a rousing welcome at the station and escort with due ceremony to the Royal Hotel. Ball heard of these preparations and alighting at the station before Hoylake walked home alone along the deserted foreshore.

This modesty was not assumed but formed part of his nature. It seemed that when playing the presence of a large gallery did not disturb him. In the heat of the fray he was oblivious of its existence, but when the strain ended he withdrew into his shell at the thought of facing an acclaiming crowd. His only rival was Harold Hilton, the second member of the famous Hoylake Triumvirate whose record of winning both the Open and Amateur Championships on two occasions, plus the American Amateur Championship, would have made him the outstanding player of his period had he not clashed with the era of Ball's greatness.

I recall the last appearance in the Amateur Championship of these grand old players. Both had ninety-nine matches to their credit in this event. Everybody hoped that the sweetness of one more victory might fall to their lot in their final championship. It was not to be. Both were defeated, and having reached the century mark their championship careers drew to a close. John Ball has gone from our midst, but to many of the older generation the mention of his name will stir memories of a silent golfer with a slight stoop striding across the Hoylake links in the dusk of a summer evening followed by his wizened little caddie.

Embryonic Champions

The world of golf in about the 1870s produced many who were to become champions. Had we visited Westward Ho and walked by the house where Amyas Leigh was born, we might have seen or heard close at hand a bland infant uninteresting in helplessness that one day would be J. H.

34

Taylor. At the same time in the village of Grouville, a few miles from St Helier, Jersey, another robust baby had arrived, the future Harry Vardon. A journey to the Fifeshire coast of Earlsferry would have revealed James Braid reclining in the same state of infantile expostulation. Freddie Tait, aged two years, had been introduced to the old garden opposite their house in George Square, Edinburgh, and perhaps that summer, during the Tait's usual family visit to St Andrews, he crawled for the first time in the sand that flanks the Old Course. Hilton was toddling round a West Kirby garden, a stone's throw from the Hoylake links. Sidney Fry, likewise bearing three years on his shoulders, was exercising his legs on the other side of the Mersey. Sandy Herd had attained the dignity of four years. Had we watched carefully by the Royal and Ancient clubhouse we might have noticed a child swinging a miniature driver. It would be Edward Blackwell, aged six years. As their home was by the first tee and home green, the boys almost lived on the links from infancy. Edward Blackwell recorded that one of the first professionals he ever saw was Davie Strath, that was because the dour golfer had fallen in love with the family nursemaid.

The year 1872 would have been too early for us to have paid our respects to such golfers as John Graham, Osmund Scott or Herman de Zoete, for, as Topsy said, they 'never was born'. But Tom Vardon had just come into the world, as also had Rowland Jones in St Helens, Isle of Wight. John Ball, as I predicted earlier, was a promising lad of nine years, whilst Horace Hutchinson had celebrated his thirteen years by winning a competition arranged by his uncle for boys under fourteen and gained the prize of a driver and cleek. J. Laidlay was meantime gaining impressions of the game as a fag at Loretto School through carrying clubs for a golfing prefect, a ritual that ended by Laidlay hurrying on ahead to make toast for this unknown young gentleman's tea. This routine laid the foundation for Laidlay's keenness for the game. His headmaster made a rule that no boy was to use an iron or cleek until he had gone round the course in fifty strokes. After a few terms at school, Laidlay qualified for this coveted honour, and the club was purchased from Old Willie Park at Musselburgh. This cleek head was attached to many shafts and became a favourite weapon during his golfing career. Had we visited the family estate near North Berwick we might have seen one of the gardeners, shortly to be the father of a boy, Jack White, who became so well known among golfers.

We would have been too early to see the Open Champion-to-be of 1904, but we might have met Robert Ferguson, who, six years earlier, had come into prominence through winning the Leith Tournament at the age of eighteen from such men as Jamie Anderson, Bob Andrews, Tom Hunter and Old Willie Park. His prize of £10 was gained with a score of 131 for four rounds of seven holes, playing throughout with borrowed clubs. The event of 1872, however, came on 13 September when the Open Championship was reinstituted and reconstituted at Prestwick. The competition had not been held since 1870 through the Challenge Belt, presented by the Earl of Eglinton, becoming the property of Young Tom Morris after winning three times in succession. Eight golfers entered. At the close their figures were:

	1st round	2nd round	3rd round	Total
Tom Morris, Jr	57	56	53	166
Davie Strath	56	52	61	169
Mr W. Doleman	63	60	54	177
Tom Morris, Sen	62	60	57	179
Davie Park	61	57	61	179
Charlie Hunter	60	60	69	189
Hugh Brown	65	73	61	199
Mr William Hunter	65	63	74	202

We would have watched Young Tom Morris win his last championship, described by Lord Justice General as 'the greatest golfer of his day'.

Edward Blackwell

These small vignettes touch on the earliest beginnings of some of the giants of the past. Each man hit the headlines. Edward Blackwell was of their number as one of the longest and most powerful drivers the game has known. He used to recall seeing such golfers as Young Tom Morris and Davie Strath. The connection was somewhat thin. The link with Strath had nothing to do with golf. Apparently he fancied Blackwell's nanny and most of the courting took place with the infant in the perambulator, an early introduction to the facts of life. Tom Morris he recalled by his Scottish bonnet and slashing style. Other remote names recalled included Robert Clark, Henry Lamb, David Lamb, Gilbert Mitchell-Innes and Freddie Tait, a few years his junior.

The span of Blackwell's life outlived his fame. The next generation knew only names like Jones, Hagen and Cotton, to be followed by Nicklaus,

Watson, and Player. Power golfers are always highlighted by their contemporaries. Prodigious distances achieved from the tee are invariably described as the longest ever. Edward Blackwell would have given any of them a run for their money, at least in driving. The figures shown in the records are staggering when we remember they were established with gutta-percha balls. With the modern ball, the shots would have been even more impressive.

Blackwell was a product of St Andrews. He was born in the university town in 1866. His home was on the verge of the Old Course and his father was a keen golfer. At the age of five he was given a roughly made driver, minus both bone and lead, and he described how he used to swing it on the grass by the Martyr's Monument. At the age of eight he attended Dr Browning's school and his first round proper at St Andrews was during a competition for the pupils of the school. Walter Blackwell won with 104: Edward was second with 108. At Glenalmond he played on the small course laid out on the cricket fields. Play was allowed only from summer to Christmas. During the holidays he returned to St Andrews, where his usual companion was Freddie Tait, to whom he gave a half. He carried only three clubs: driver, iron and cleek. The last named was used as a putter with the resulting habit of stabbing at the ball instead of following through. In spite of these habits he was a scratch golfer at the age of eighteen.

In 1885 he left Glenalmond and returned to St Andrews. Shortly afterwards H. B. Simpson of Barnton arranged a match between Blackwell and Jack Simpson, the reigning Open Champion. After thirty-six holes Blackwell won by a single hole. Nine days later he left for America and was away for six years without touching a golf club. On returning to St Andrews he won the William IV Medal at the Autumn Meeting with the record return of 82. That winter he returned to the States and was a further five years away without playing. The break did not affect his play. When he came back he won the Calcutta Cup from plus two. In the spring of 1898 Blackwell went to Pau and brought his handicap to plus five. In partnership with Charles Hutchings he won the Kilmaine Cup for Pau against Biarritz. The records usually isolate Edward Blackwell's performance in the 1904 Amateur Championship at Sandwich when he was beaten by W. J. Travis in the final. It is said that Travis won through inspired putting. Blackwell always disagreed. He said the reason was the moving of the tees to a more forward position which cancelled his advantage over the shorter-driving American.

As regards his appearance, Horace Hutchinson left a vivid word portrait: 'Standing above six feet in height, his physique shows the very perfection of strength. Not only is he well endowed but his strength is something altogether out of the common, and it is strength of that special quality that is capable of being exerted in rapid movement. It is doubtless this union of activity and power, combined with the ideal orthodoxy of his style, that gives him his tremendous length of drive.' With such flowery style, it would have been interesting to speculate what Hutchinson might have written about Nicklaus.

Judging by photographs Blackwell's style could hardly be described as orthodox. At the top of the swing his right elbow was raised at an unusual height but this was in line with the theories of the older school. He adopted the St Andrews swing, yet the club was rarely below the horizontal behind the back. He was an individualist. He tried and rejected the Vardon interlocking grip with the right thumb down the shaft. He never had professional coaching. The rudiments were given by his father, after that he developed his own style.

His best drives were made with gutta-percha balls. In 1892 while playing the fifth hole at St Andrews, measuring about 520 yards, he reached the green in two shots with the wind slightly against in a match with Major Robert Bethune. Turning round, he played the same hole going in, about 500 yards, and again reached the green with his second. In four gutta-percha shots he had driven more than a thousand yards. A few years later he drove from the eighteenth tee on the Old Course to the steps on the left of the green. His longest single drive measured by tape was in 1892 from the seventeenth tee. It was 366 yards. The significant thing about all these lusty drives was the fact that they were not with rubber-cored balls but the less responsive gutta-percha.

5

Age of the Morris Era

NINETEENTH-CENTURY golfers tend to be shadowy figures with occasional strong personalities bridging the gulf between the centuries. One such was Tom Morris, whose record was outstanding. Not only did he achieve fame before newspaper reports made all men indistinguishable, but his life span was so long he outlived most of his contemporaries. He was born on 16 June 1821, in North Street, St Andrews. His father, John Morris, was employed as a letter-carrier. His mother, Jean Bruce, came from Anstruther. He grew up in an atmosphere of golf and began to play with a rough-carved miniature club when he was six. It was a world totally remote from today. Topics discussed in general conversation belong to a time capsule but were a background to the years when Morris was a pupil at Madras College. George IV had died the year before Tom was born. Alexander I, Tsar of Russia, had been succeeded by his brother, Nicholas, four years earlier. Napoleon Bonaparte died in 1821 on St Helena. James Monroe was President of the United States of America. The first steam-boat crossed the Atlantic, but the Liverpool–Manchester Railway had yet to be opened. It was a period enriched by such men as Wordsworth, Beethoven, Sir Walter Scott, Charles Lamb and Sir Robert Peel. John Keats had died in 1821. Tom Cribb was Champion of England after an epic bare-knuckle fight. Gustavus, a 'shabby little grey', bought for 25 guineas at Hampton Court, won the 1821 Derby and a prize of £1,758.15s, while John Welles had been 'no-balled' for using round-arm bowling.

Such were current affairs when Tom Morris was born. They were years of far-reaching change, like that day in March 1891 when the first London to Paris telephone was opened and the revival a few months later of the

Olympic Games proposed by Baron de Courbertin; the historic moment in June 1896 when Guglielimo Marconi sent a message over a mile by wireless; the discovery of radium by Marie and Pierre Curie in 1898; Thomas Edison's invention of the electric battery; the Wright brothers' first flight in 1903 by a heavier-than-air craft, followed six years later by Bleriot becoming the first to cross the Channel by aeroplane – epic moments that today are taken for granted. The Open Championship trophy may be hurtled across the Atlantic in the luggage of Jack Nicklaus but in the Morris heyday such an occurrence would have been like space fiction, yet throughout these formative decades this trophy has remained the prized object of golfing ambition.

Tom Morris's link with the game took shape at eighteen when he was apprenticed to Allan Robertson in the ball-making trade. The association was satisfactory until Morris played in that match in which a gutta-percha ball was used. Fearful of the new ball affecting the feathery-ball trade, the two men had a row. Morris quit and set up a similar business on his own. In 1851 Colonel Fairlie invited Morris to take a job at Prestwick that involved looking after the Links. He accepted and stayed for fourteen years. During that time history was made. The Prestwick Club inaugurated an Open Tournament in 1860 with a Championship Belt as a prize. Willie Park won the first event. Morris took the next two and repeated the success in 1864 and 1867. He competed in every Open up to and including 1896, the year that Harry Vardon won his first title.

Major Boothby was anxious to tempt Morris back to St Andrews. He proposed at a General Meeting of the Royal and Ancient Club that a first-class professional should be employed as a Servant of the Club to take entire charge of the golf course. The suggestion was approved. A salary of £50 a year was fixed, the appointment coming under the jurisdiction of the Green Committee. On 9 January 1865, Tom Morris attended a full meeting of members in the Clubhouse. The duties were spelt out and Tom could employ a man to do the heavy work, like carting, for two days a week. Upon accepting the post, Morris was formally handed the tools of the job – a barrow, spade and shovel.

For the next forty-four years Morris spent his life in St Andrews, gaining a reputation that was respected throughout the golfing world. In June 1903 he resigned as greenkeeper but was made Honorary Greenkeeper with the assurance that his salary of £50 per annum would be continued for the rest of his life. Further tangible recognition was the collection of over £1,000 and the purchase of an annuity of £80 a year. Sir George

Reid, President of the Royal Scottish Academy, was commissioned by the Royal and Ancient Golf Club members to paint Morris' picture. The finished portrait hangs in the Club and was first exhibited in August 1903. In his eighty-seventh year Morris had a fall in the New Club and never fully recovered. He died in May 1908. On the day of his funeral there was no play on the Links, an imaginative gesture. Tom Morris was, and his memory still is, a symbol of the game.

Like the rest of us, Tom Morris had his tragedies. One that hit hard was the death of his son. Young Tom was born at Prestwick in 1851. He took to golf as naturally as his father had done and made his first public appearance at a tournament in Perth when only thirteen years of age. Considered too young to compete in the main event, he was matched against Master William Greig, who was described as a juvenile golfing celebrity. A contemporary report tells all:

The most interesting match of the day was between Master Morris, son of the redoubtable Tom, and Master Greig of Perth. The latter played with astonishing neatness and precision, but the honours of the day were in store for his competitor. Master Morris seems to have been born and bred to golf. He has been cast in the very mould of a golfer and plays with all the steadiness and certainty of his father. It was funny to see the boys followed by hundreds of deeply interested and anxious spectators.

The reporter was quick to spot a potential champion.

In 1867 Young Tom came of age in a golfing sense, for although only sixteen he tied for the first place with Willie Park and Bob Andrews in a tournament at Carnoustie which attracted all the professionals. Young Tom won the play-off by two shots from Andrews with a card of 132. Park trailed well behind. Bob Andrews was to Perth what Tom Morris was to St Andrews. Born in 1835, he was known as The Rook, and played many matches against the Morrisses, father and son. In one of these against Morris senior at Prestwick, he holed out in two to win the match by a fluke. His drive, with the club known as the Black Doctor, was too strong, scattered the spectators round the green, struck a top hat and rebounded on to the green within inches of the hole.

In 1867 Young Tom made his debut in the Open Championship. He finished fourth behind his father, who won the Belt and £8 prize money. The following year Young Tom made no mistake. He won the Belt with 154 and a margin of eleven strokes, and repeated the feat in 1869 with 157 and the same margin. He made the Championship Belt his own property in 1870 with a third consecutive win, this by twelve strokes with a total of 149. Prestwick in those days was a 12-hole course and the Championship was decided over three rounds with par for the course being 49. The margin of these three wins emphasizes Young Tom's superiority over his contemporaries. The third victory showed an average of $74\frac{1}{2}$ per round and was unbeaten in the Championship as long as the guttie was used, and the entries included such men as J. H. Taylor, Harry Vardon and James Braid. It was only beaten 34 years later by Jack White at Sandwich.

After Young Tom made the Championship Belt his own property at the age of nineteen, the Open Championship itself was reviewed. After an interregnum of one year, no Championship being held in 1871, a Silver Cup was presented by the Royal and Ancient Golf Club, Prestwick Golf Club and the Honourable Company of Edinburgh Golfers as a permanent trophy, the winner to receive a Gold Medal. The Championship was to be played at Prestwick, St Andrews and Musselburgh in rotation, the three Clubs sharing management of the event. Prestwick staged the 1872 Open and once again Young Tom won in bad weather with an aggregate seventeen strokes higher than in 1870.

Without doubt Young Tom was the finest golfer of his time. As regards technique, it is difficult to get a clear picture. Photographs are scarce, but contemporary comments suggest a swing that was not as full as the traditional sweeping St Andrews style, not as rhythmic as Davie Strath's. In spite of pronounced muscular shoulders, he lacked length but compensated with a body action so forceful that at times shafts were broken. This forcing thrust helped in recovery shots from bad lies. His iron shots were outstanding. He introduced the niblick, later the mashie or five-iron, for approach shots. Its value had been demonstrated by Allan Robertson, and Young Tom used it to good effect in a series of matches against Arthur Molesworth, the Westward Ho amateur. On a frostbound course with a small area of each green cleared of snow, Young Tom continually pitched the ball up to the pin knowing that the backspin would make it stop. He played these shots with an open stance rather than with the ball nearer the left foot. On the greens he had an upright stance, used a wooden putter and played the ball almost off the right toe with the left toe pointing at the hole. No weakness was apparent in any of his shot-making.

Everything pointed to a long, brilliant career, when everything changed overnight. He was playing with his father in a challenge match at North Berwick against the brothers, Willie and Mungo Park, when a telegram was delivered to the clubhouse. It said that Young Tom's wife was danger-

An historic moment when Lord Balfour drove the ball that made him Captain of the Royal and Ancient Golf Club, applauded by the veteran Old Tom Morris. His partner, Graham Murray, is on the right. Appreciative spectators show the fashions of the day. Balfour's caddy carries a limited range of clubs.

Mungo Park, member of the famous Park family and Argentine Open Champion in 1905, 1907 and 1912.

ously ill. Provost Brodie decided not to hand it over until the match ended. A yacht belonging to John Lewis, an Edinburgh golfer, was put at the disposal of the Morrisses. By crossing the Firth of Forth, they were saved the railway journey through Edinburgh. As they walked from the harbour, a second telegram brought the news that his wife had died in childbirth. Young Tom never recovered from the shock. Three months later he had dinner with a few friends on Christmas Eve and retired to bed, but died in his sleep on Christmas Day 1875 at the age of twenty-four.

Soon after his death a memorial to his memory was made possible by public subscription. The committee accepted the design by John Rhind, the Edinburgh sculptor, worked out in Bibby Freestone. In bas-relief, a figure of Young Tom, about three-quarter life-size, is shown in golf jacket and wearing a Scottish Glengarry. He addresses the ball with an iron, sizing up a wrist shot to the hole. The inscription was written by the Very Reverend Principal Tulloch, Dean of the Thistle and Vice-Chancellor of the University of St Andrews: 'In memory of "Tommy", son of Thomas Morris, who died 25th December 1875, aged twenty-four years. Deeply regretted by numerous friends and all golfers. He thrice in succession won the Champion Belt and held it without rivalry, and yet without envy, his many amiable qualities being no less acknowledged than his golfing achievements. This monument has been erected by contributions from sixty golfing societies.' The memorial was unveiled on 25 September 1878 by Miss Phelps, on behalf of Mrs Hunter, Young Tom's sister.

It is impossible to compare performances of one generation with those of another. It is enough to say that talent begets talent, but genius is unique.

The Park Era

Another golfer who exercised enormous influence in the early days was Willie Park. If reputations are any guide, one of the greatest putters of all time was Willie Park, Jr. Dispensing words of wisdom about the art of putting, he never underestimated his domination. 'I give all the knowledge that won for me the position of the best and most consistent putter in the world – I was highly successful and the great strength of my game was my ability to hole, with certainty, putts from two to three yards.' If only Sandy Lyle had such belief in his ability. Park spoke as a member of the famous golfing family of Musselburgh. His father won the Championship Belt in the inaugural event of 1860 and again in 1863 and 1866. After

Young Tom Morris won the Belt three times in succession, the familiar Open trophy was won by Willie's uncle, Mungo, in 1874. It was Park senior's turn in 1875, with young Willie taking the title in 1887 and 1899.

When J. H. Taylor of Winchester became the first English professional to win the Championship five years later, Willie challenged 'J. H.' to a man-to-man match and beat him, much to the satisfaction of Scotsmen who resented English intrusion. Park's putter, shallow-faced, wry-necked and slightly lofted, had a long shaft so designed to cope with cuppy lies. Favouring a stance in front of the ball, his advice was clear: 'I keep the club just clear of the ground. I hit only the ball, never the ball and the ground, and by keeping the club clear of the ground, I hit the ball high on its centre, thus making it keep close to the ground on the way to the hole.'

His stance was distinctive. He stood with his left foot completely withdrawn, the ball only five inches from and just in front of his right toe. The club was held at the bottom of the grip. He crouched over the ball and used only his wrists. He said he never saw the hole when he hit the ball and never looked up until it had time to drop in the hole. One thing is certain. The method worked on greens that were nothing like the current velvety finish. Given such conditions, Willie might have been even more successful.

Laurie and Willie Auchterlonie

Another old golfing family of the distant past was the Auchterlonies. Of five brothers, all of whom were keen golfers, two were outstanding. The eldest, Laurence, was born in St Andrews in 1868. He decided to work in America and for several years was professional at the Glenview Club. His eventful year was 1902 when he entered for the United States Open Championship at Garden City, Long Island. Increased prize money attracted an entry of ninety with the bait of 200 dollars for the winner and 970 dollars shared among the first ten places. Auchterlonie liked the new ball which had been developed jointly by Goodrich Company and the Cleveland amateur named Coburn Haskell. The hard rubber core had added some twenty yards to a drive. Auchterlonie's four rounds of 78-78-74-77 not only won the title, but for the first time the winner had broken 80 in all four rounds. In second place came Walter J. Travis, the leading American amateur of that time, and designer of the Garden City course.

Willie Auchterlonie won the 1893 Open Championship with equipment of seven clubs. In 1950 he accepted Honorary Membership of the Royal and Ancient Golf Club along with J. H. Taylor and James Braid. He died in 1964 aged 91.

A couple of years later, Travis became the first American to win the British Amateur Championship. Laurence Auchterlonie returned home to St Andrews and finished second in the Scottish Professional Championship of 1919.

Willie Auchterlonie, born in St Andrews in 1872, played in the Open for the first time at the age of sixteen, when Jack Burns won the title over the Old Course from an entry of 53 with an aggregate of 171. Five years later, it was his turn to win the Championship with a total of 322. Auchterlonie's equipment consisted of a set of seven clubs he had made himself. Provided a player had mastered the technique of the half, three-quarter and full shots, they were more than adequate. Not long afterwards, he began the famous St Andrews clubmaking company. In that 1893 Open his winning aggregate of 322 had been followed by J. E. Laidlay – 324; Sandy Herd – 325; Hugh Kirkaldy – 326; Andrew Kirkaldy – also 326; with Old Tom Morris on 383. Virtually the same entry went to Newcastle, Co. Down for the Irish Open Championship. Willie Auchterlonie was again the winner with 322. Sandy Herd finished with 325; Hugh and Andrew Kirkaldy tied on 326; J. H. Taylor on 333; Ben Sayers 335; Harry Vardon 334; Tom Vardon 345; Old Tom Morris 383. Willie Auchterlonie was appointed Royal and Ancient professional in September 1935 and carried out his duties with courteous efficiency. He laid out the eighteen-hole Jubilee Course at St Andrews, which was opened in 1946. In 1950 he accepted Honorary Membership of the Royal and Ancient Golf Club, along with James Braid and J. H. Taylor. He died in 1964 aged ninety-one, the Auchterlonie tradition being continued when his son, Laurie, an expert clubmaker, was appointed R and A professional.

Andra Kirkaldy

The reference to Andrew Kirkaldy recalls a rare character who larded his presence in the game's annals. He was better known to an older generation as Andra, the natural successor to Old Tom Morris. He was known for his native pawkiness, the Fife accent which English ears found somewhat difficult, and a shrewd wit. He was a link between the old and new school of professionals. I recall his comment when our Walker Cup team had a severe drubbing. 'There's nae muckle wrang with the team. They are a' fit tae win if they are on their game. Gowfers the day are saw muckle in and out ye never can tell when they are going tae be on their game or no. The hale trouble lies in the ba'. The gutta ba' wis aye reliable and ye could

Andrew Kirkaldy, who succeeded Old Tom Morris. He was the link between the old and new school of professionals.

easy enough pick the best gowfers, but its no the case today, for I tell ye the ba' beats the gowfer.' Although many years have passed, I can still picture the old professional seated in state by the home green during an Open Championship. If there was any doubt as to where he was, he could be located by the steady stream of pertinent observations upon golf matters in general. As each couple came up, he would rise from his chair until the business of holing out was finished. He would then retire to his chair until the next couple appeared over the Swilcan Bridge. I remember him describing in his closing years what he regarded as the two greatest surprises of his life. First, when he saw 70 broken in a Championship on the Old Course; second, when a professional walked across his line of vision resplendent in dinner jacket and studded shirt-front. The spectacle was a constant topic of disdain and amazement. He was indeed a rich personality. There was only one Andra. There will never be another.

From its inauguration in 1860 the Open has known spells of domination. The Morrises, father and son, and the Parks shared the honours until the years of the famous triumvirate plus one. The first to appear was Alexander (Sandy) Herd in 1868. James Braid entered the world in February 1870, followed three months later by Harry Vardon born in Jersey. The following year John Henry Taylor made his debut in North Devon. Between them they won the Open seventeen times. Sandy's tally was one, but he finished six times in the first three. In 1926 he won the Match-play Championship for the second time at the age of fifty-eight. In the late 'nineties he beat Harry Vardon twice in match-play clashes when Vardon was at the crest of his success. Sandy's last appearance in the Open was 1939 at the age of seventy-one. He had the longest competitive career of the four. When he died in 1944 I felt the game had lost one of the few remaining giants of the last century.

Sandy Herd

There were several distinctive features about Herd's game, particularly his waggle. It did not indicate indecision, but was a process of deciding the right psychological moment to strike the ball. He used the old-fashioned palm grip instead of the then popular interlock or overlap. His favourite shot was a cut-up with a spoon. The last time I played with him was in a practice round before the 1936 Open Championship at Hoylake. The course was long and the wind blew strongly (tiring conditions for a man of his age), the waggles decreased, his long game introduced an extra full shot, but direction was impeccable. The cunning hook for which he was famous was very much in evidence.

Herd's golfing service was spent with three clubs, Huddersfield, Coombe Hill and Moor Park, but at heart he was a product of St Andrews. Born in a humble house in North Street on 24 April 1868, he used to say that his introduction to the game was not on the links, but in North Street. The childhood links stretched to Bell Street. Holes were lampposts which had to be hit by balls made from champagne corks. One of his companions was Laurence Auchterlonie. Childish ambitions came true: Laurie went to America and won the US title, and Sandy had the same success in this country. His professional career began through David Lamb. Herd was working as a plasterer for Andrew Scott, whose yard produced three Open Champions. Lamb received a message asking him to find a professional for the summer months at Portrush. Herd accepted and started in 1890. So began a golfing career that was to be brilliant. He won the Open Championship at Hoylake in 1902 and was runner-up on four occasions. The record should be assessed by remembering that for many years he had to play against the best ball of Vardon, Taylor and Braid. Herd's Open victory marked the arrival of the rubber-cored ball. A month earlier the Amateur Championship had been staged over the same links. The potential of the Haskell ball was demonstrated when Charles Hutchings narrowly beat Sidney Fry in a storm of wind and rain. Even so the professionals were unimpressed. The new ball was rejected for the gutta-percha. Herd was of their number until that practice round with John Ball. The Hoylake amateur, using a Haskell, beat the professional by such a margin that Herd had second thoughts and switched to the new ball for the Open. It was a wise choice. Vardon finished one stroke behind Herd, who almost lost through over-anxiety in the closing holes. It was this tendency to panic when under pressure that prevented him from repeating the Open breakthrough. When he was able to control ragged nerves, some of his early enthusiasm had waned. Even so, he finished second to George Duncan in the 1920 Open at the age of fifty-two, a tragic 7 at the 16th cost the title. Six years later he won the *News of the World* Tournament, the equivalent of the PGA Matchplay Championship, on the 38th green after a terrific struggle in appalling weather. I pick 1895 as his best year. He is remembered as a great golfer and a warm-hearted character.

James Braid

James Braid started life as a joiner, first at Elie, then St Andrews, later Edinburgh, and was working at his trade while J. H. Taylor and Harry Vardon were already budding professionals. About the end of 1893, a year before Taylor won his first championship, Braid switched trades and became a clubmaker. His chance to show prowess as a player came in 1895. An exhibition match staged between Braid and Taylor on a sub-urban course ended with honours even. Braid's potential was established. He finished second in the 1897 Open, beaten by Harold Hilton by a single stroke. He won the title for the first time in 1901. In the short space of a decade he claimed the championship five times.

His victories at St Andrews in 1905 and 1910 were affected by frightful weather. The entry in 1905 was 152. Rounds of 81-78-78-81 were good enough to win in spite of sixes at the 15th and 16th. On both occasions Braid drove out-of-bounds and had to play from difficult lies on the railway track. In 1910 play was disrupted by a thunderstorm leaving flooded bunkers and submerged greens. Braid completed the round in torrential rain and lightning and handed in a card of 77, which he always regarded as the finest round of his career. Sadly the Old Course was pronounced unplayable and the round was discarded. He went on to win with an aggregate of 299.

A tall, exceptionally powerful player, Braid was noted for long driving, particularly against the wind when he would attack the ball with reckless abandon, a trait maybe inherited from the likes of Douglas Rolland, another famous long hitter, who, like Braid, also came from Elie in Fife. Those who knew him will recall his long, slow stride. He was unflappable, cool, with a pawky sense of humour, always sparce with words, often preferring monosyllabic answers. He was a superb cleek player, with the hint of a slight weakness with a putter.

He held a record of returning a birthday round with a score lower than his age until his eightieth round. He failed on a wet, cold and windy February day over a bleak Walton Heath course at its unkindest. Well protected in waterproofs, Braid ignored the elements and got his figures until the last hole when the wind was so fierce he had no hope of carrying the cross-bunker to reach the green in 2. The third shot ended in a side bunker and he was obliged to settle for 81. He did a fine job as golfing architect but earned the reputation of being ruthless with bunker-siting. One of his creations at Prestwick caused J. H. Taylor to say that the man

Harry Vardon and James Braid ... giants of the last century whose long driving and extraordinary powers of recovery would have been outstanding at any period.

Allan Fullerton Macfie, the first Amateur Champion after winning the 1885 Tournament at Hoylake.

who made the bunker ought to be buried in it with a niblick through his heart.

Braid was one of the founder members of the Professional Golfers Association and the first professional to be elected an honorary member of his Club. To that distinction was added the honour of being made a member of the Royal and Ancient Golf Club, along with J. H. Taylor and Willie Auchterlonie. His last round was played on his beloved Walton Heath. Shortly afterwards he attended a PGA meeting, then entered hospital for an operation. Surgery was successful but he suffered a relapse when about to return home. Two days later he passed away on 27 November 1950 and was buried at St Peters Church at Walton-on-the-Heath.

James Braid holds a place of special fame in the history of the game.

J. H. Taylor

Temperamentally J. H. Taylor was unlike other members of the Triumvirate. James Braid had a natural dignity, reticent and kindly with a gentle exterior. Harry Vardon was quiet with a placid temperament – everything on a low key. In contrast J. H. was pugnacious and tenacious, a dour fighter on and off the course. As principal founder of the Professional Golfers Association and pioneer of public course golf in England, one of his proudest moments was when he argued his case with the Office of Works officials to play golf in Richmond Park and the Prince of Wales later opened the first of the two courses. Taylor won five Open Championships and finished second many times. A man of character, many will recall his tremendous enthusiasm and resolution. A true caricature showed a sturdy figure with massive boots anchored flat-footed to the ground, cap jammed down over his nose, chin protruding as he battled against a gale. In such conditions he was firm as a rock. As a player his swing was somewhat curtailed: right foot slightly forward, drives ruled the pin. Temperamentally there was no hint of a stoical poker-faced pose about him. Few men have had to quell such inner flames. He was a superb cleek player and a masterly mashie-artist to the pin; if criticism be allowed, there were occasional hiccups on the green.

In 1951 the BBC planned a programme recording Taylor's reminiscences. Since he was unwilling to leave the quiet of Westward Ho, the unit travelled to Devon. Technicians converted his sitting-room into a studio. The microphone was installed on a desk which J. H. told me had been presented by the Artisan Golfers' Association. During the afternoon he recalled many triumphs. High on the list were the 1895 and 1900 Open triumphs. He was proud of being the first English-born professional to win the title and recalled how it wounded Scottish pride.

He spoke of his childhood at Northam, the village by the Westward Ho links where he was born in 1871. As a lad he caddied, later working for the club professionals, Johnnie, Mat and Jamie Allan. He carried clubs regularly for Horace Hutchinson, from whom he picked up many useful tips, and talked of the day when he beat the famous amateur by one hole. He lived again the matches against Vardon, Braid and Herd, but the victory that stood out was at St Andrews in 1895. Vardon had the lowest score for the first round, but in the end could only tie for ninth place as J. H. recorded his second successive Open win. The next year Vardon had his revenge at Muirfield. Prior to that championship, Vardon played a challenge match against Taylor over 36 holes and won by 8 and 6. In the Open both men tied on 316, Vardon narrowly winning the play-off for his first Championship victory. Over the next three years, Vardon won twice more, but J. H. countered at St Andrews in 1900, becoming Champion with an aggregate of 309.

When asked what would be his choice for playing an important match, there was no hesitation in nominating St Andrews. He felt the Old Course set a stern but fair examination and demanded the right temperament. It had to be tackled intelligently, a magnificent and unique test of golfing skills. That view has been confirmed by champions of every decade.

Harry Vardon

The third member of the Triumvirate, Harry Vardon was unlike the pugnacious J. H. Taylor and the rangy, almost ungainly James Braid. In his prime Vardon was slim, quietly spoken and always dressed in knickerbockers and tweed jacket. For golfing style, he anticipated the likes of Walter Hagen and Bobby Jones, who epitomized practical smartness. Vardon created a record by winning the Open Championship six times, in 1896, 1898, 1899, 1903, 1911 and 1914. He popularized the Vardon grip. At the outset, like most golfers he used the two-handed grip with no fingers overlapping or interlocking. For the record, J. H. Taylor was the first to experiment to find a more controlled grip by adopting the overlapping method, which he used for a time at Westward Ho, but Vardon persevered. In the aftermath to his run of Open successes, the grip was universally accepted. It should be pointed out that the amateur J. E. Laidlay favoured this grip several years earlier.

Harry Vardon was born in a cottage not far from the Grouville links in Jersey on 9 May 1870 and died at Totteridge on 20 March 1937. At the zenith of his game he played like the genius he was, particularly with the guttie. His upright swing helped to strike the ball high and clean from almost any kind of lie. He was particularly long and was expert at placing a high-floating, abruptly stopping brassy shot within holing distance in 2 as against two full shots and a chip needed by most opponents. He was also famed for accurate push-shots with a cleek. Such was the consistent quality of shot-making that he dominated the golfing world, influence that marked his American tour and victory in the United States Open. He did more than anyone to popularize the game on the other side of the Atlantic. The break caused by the First World War brought to a close Vardon's championship career, but nothing could detract from his achievements. For some time he was handicapped by illness and had a spell in a sanatorium, but though playing was curtailed, his enthusiasm was un-diminished. Attempts have been made to compare him with Bobby Jones and Walter Hagen, Ben Hogan and Jack Nicklaus, even Nick Faldo. It is tempting but pointless to make such comparisons. I can only say that a golfer can only be the outstanding player of his day. Beyond that is not possible. I might add that Harry Vardon regarded the closing years of the nineteenth century as the golden age of the game.

A. F. Macfie

Leaving the heyday of the Triumvirate, it is interesting to recall some of the amateur giants of that period. I took a photograph of Allan Fullerton Macfie outside the Royal and Ancient clubhouse. It is now an historic link with the remote past. Macfie was a dominant figure in that eventful tournament held at Hoylake in April 1885. The idea, mooted by Thomas Owen Potter at a Council Meeting of the Royal Liverpool Golf Club, resolved that 'a Tournament open to all Amateur golfers should be held at Hoylake in the Spring Meeting Week of 1885.' The committee appointed to oversee the event consisted of James Cullen, B. Hall Blyth, F. C. Mansfield, John Dun, J. Logan White, F. C. Cranford, Charles D. Brown, T. O. Potter and Horace Hutchinson.

Little did these nine gentlemen realize what the future would be for this competition which attracted forty-eight entries from the Royal and

Ancient, Royal Liverpool, Blackheath, Royal Wimbledon, Honourable Company of Edinburgh Golfers, New Club, North Berwick, Glasgow, Earlsferry and Elie, Dalhousie, Carnoustie, Worcestershire and London Scottish. Entrance fee was fixed at one guinea. Prizes were donated by the Royal Liverpool Golf Club. All was harmony and accord except for the technical nicety as to what constituted an *amateur* and, more to the point, to get a clearer definition of a *professional*. The query arose because of an entry received from Douglas Rolland. After finishing second to Jack Simpson in the Open Championship of 1884, Rolland had accepted prize money, and in so doing broke the rule forbidding amateurs to receive a financial reward when competing against professionals. The ruling was straightforward until it was pointed out that some years earlier at an Open Championship, John Ball, then a lad, had finished in the money-winning list and had accepted a prize of ten shillings. Technically the Rolland issue was clear-cut, but the embarrassing possibility that Ball might lose his amateur status because of this action seemed absurd. Horace Hutchinson anticipated that the Council would reject Rolland's entry, was reluctant to become involved, particularly as Rolland was rated his main opponent, and formally resigned before the vote was taken. The entry was disallowed. Guile helped to solve the other headache. As Ball's slip had occurred before he was sixteen, his amateur status was deemed still intact.

In the tournament, byes were not limited in the first round so there was only one semi-final. John Ball Tertius began his championship career by beating Colonel Kinnard by 8 and 7. His father, John Ball, Jr, also won his match against G. A. Gilroy, which meant that father and son met in the third round, with the youth winning on the sixteenth green. In the fourth round Macfie had a tough match against De Zoete and won only after extra holes with Macfie holing the Rushes in one, victory ensuring a place in the semi-final where he received a bye. The other semi-final between Horace Hutchinson and John Ball Tertius was a see-saw affair. Ball, two up at the turn, looked the stronger player, but Hutchinson rallied, became dormy two up, only to lose the seventeenth when he drove out of bounds. He made no mistake at the eighteenth, leaving his iron shot dead and won by two holes. Hutchinson was expected to crush Macfie in the final, but the Scot refused to be overawed, winning the first four holes, eventually trouncing the favourite by 7 and 6.

Afterwards, in response to a request made in January 1886 by Hall Byth, the Hoylake captain, to the Royal and Ancient Club, it was decided that a competition should be held over three links in rotation, St Andrews,

Hoylake and Prestwick. A piece of plate valued at £100 was bought with money subscribed by the twenty-four leading Clubs and the winner was also to receive a Gold Medal. The outcome was the staging of the first Amateur Championship on the Old Course, St Andrews, in September 1886.

There were ten matches in the first round, sixteen in the second. Macfie lost to J. E. Laidlay in the third round, who in turn was beaten by Ball Tertius in the next. Horace Hutchinson defeated H. A. Lamb in the final by 7 and 6 over eighteen holes. The thirty-six-hole test did not come in until 1896. After the First World War, the Royal and Ancient Club ruled that the 1885 Tournament at Hoylake should be recognized as the first Amateur Championship, which meant that A. F. Macfie was proclaimed the first Amateur Champion, a recognition immensely valued by the Scot.

Allan Macfie was a familiar figure in Hoylake and St Andrews for many years, walking slowly across the fairways, cap well down over the eyes, drooping moustaches and cleek in hand. As a golfer, his game lacked length. He used to say that he had never been over the Swilcan Burn in two shots at the first, but at short range his accuracy more than compensated. Caddies, arriving early, often found the fairway littered with balls left behind after he had given up practising in the fading light of the previous evening. The first Amateur Champion was a member of the Royal and Ancient Golf Club for sixty-one years.

He showed a lively interest in the game up to the end of his life. In shot-making he was a perfectionist. 'I do not suppose,' Harold Hilton wrote, 'that any player living practised the game so assidiously as Allan Macfie did in those old days at Hoylake. He was full of theories and maintained that to make the ball rise abruptly, the eye had to be fixed on the ground immediately in front of the ball. It suited him, but imitators ran foul of topping.'

Horace Hutchinson

Macfie was the forerunner of some outstanding amateurs, champions like John Ball and Harold Hilton, whose feats I have described elsewhere in this book; Horace Hutchinson, who exercised considerable influence in the development of golf in England, was a true pioneer with a flamboyant personality but at times temperamental. He would have been outstanding in any decade. Like J. H. Taylor he took to golf as a boy at Westward Ho. Purists criticized his habit of raising the right elbow and dipping the right knee. Maybe they were potential faults, but results soon silenced the critics. Somehow those early golfers were far more charismatic than their successors. It was the age of the individual, warts and all. There was more artistry about their shot-making. A bag of seven clubs could cope with any situation. Of this company of pioneers, I single out three who were real champions.

Freddie Tait

Some years ago the championship scene was enlivened by the sight of 'Arnie's Army' sweeping across the fairways in support of Arnold Palmer, an American who was in a category of his own. Golfing skill was his instinctive nature. He won every honour and in the process held the affection of the golfing public. It is hard to describe his influence on the game unless you had first felt the impact of his personality. The same could be said of Freddie Tait, a name unfamiliar today, but outstanding in the last decade of the nineteenth century. He was Scotland's greatest amateur, literally a national hero, with an enthusiastic following. England was the enemy when it came to golf, and preferably the battleground had to be St Andrews. He never won the Open Championship, though came very close on several occasions, but excelled in match play. In his first Amateur Championship win, he beat J. E. Laidlay, John Ball, Horace Hutchinson and Harold Hilton in the final in 1896. Throughout his playing career he continually came up against either Ball or Hilton. The latter he invariably beat, but Ball had the edge on him, probably because the Hoylake man was the better player. He did not favour the extreme slashing style associated with Fife but took the club back slowly and under control. Very long from the tee, some of his drives contradicted the theories put forward by his father, an eminent St Andrews professor of physics, who had firm views how far a ball could travel. Tait would have nothing to do with the popular Vardon grip but held the club in old-fashioned manner with the right hand well underneath the shaft. He was adept at the pitch-and-run and putted with a pronounced lofted cleek that lifted the ball slightly in the air. He could be erratic, playing a crooked shot into all sorts of trouble. His powers of recovery from seemingly hopeless lies would have made Ballesteros green with envy. He enjoyed his golf and spectators shared his evident pleasure. An officer in the Black Watch, he volunteered for active service in South Africa. He was only thirty when

Freddie Tait lines up a putt against John Ball in the Amateur Championship at St Andrew's. Tait, who was killed in the South African War, enjoyed popularity in Scotland on a par with Ball's hero-worship at Hoylake.

J. Mure Fergusson had a distinctive style on the green, upright stance, and played the ball off the right foot. He is watched by J. E. Laidlay, a formidable cleek player. He was the first player to use an overlap grip.

he was killed at Koodoosberg Drift and was buried by the side of the Riet River. He achieved a great deal in a short time.

J. E. Laidlay

J. E. Laidlay is even less known today, but during the same period was a dominant force in amateur golf. He won the Amateur Championship twice, was three times runner-up, and narrowly missed winning the Open in 1893. Born at Seacliff, Haddingtonshire in 1860, Laidlay went to Loretto School at the age of twelve and took to golf two years later. The records were sprinkled with Laidlay rounds which in those days were remarkably low. At Musselburgh in 1876 in a three-ball match, he carded the two rounds in 72. St Andrews, Hoylake and Carnoustie were played in 77. At North Berwick he returned 70 with an outward half that included one two and six threes. Luffness was completed in 69. Today such scores would be commonplace, but the equipment and balls then used, plus the state of the links, made such low scoring outstanding. His style was unorthodox in that he drew his weight away from the ball in the backswing, bringing it back at impact. It suited him, but must have been hopeless to copy. Apart from golf, Laidlay made his mark at cricket. At sixteen he played for the Gentlemen of Scotland against Yorkshire and claimed eleven county wickets for 73 with his slow bowling, prowess that would have been approved by the likes of Leonard Crawley and Ted Dexter.

Francis Ouimet

The name of Francis Ouimet was known and respected on both sides of the Atlantic for many years. The span covered several decades. One end went back to the Country Club at Brookline, Massachusetts, in 1913 when Ouimet figured in the memorable tie for the American Open Championship with Harry Vardon and Ted Ray. The other end might be said to touch St Andrews in 1951, when he was officially installed as Captain of the Royal and Ancient Club. The years between were crammed with golfing incident and achievement, but in retrospect it is interesting to pinpoint the man apart from his golfing feats. The bespectacled American did not conform to the usual transatlantic reaction to headline success. He did not attempt to combine the wit of a jester with the skill of a genius. Ouimet was more at home with English conservatism than with American showmanship. His career took a different pattern to many of his countrymen. Take Walter

Hagen as an example. He started as a novelty and became an institution. Ouimet began as an unknown amateur and came to fame overnight as Open Champion. He matured into a senior statesman of the game, yet throughout remained unassuming and modest to the point of self-effacement.

Ouimet was a curious mixture, a bundle of extremes. Bobby Jones recorded one of their championship matches: 'Francis was solemn as a judge: he always is in a match.' The description was apt. There was always an air of solemnity about Ouimet's play. On the other hand, it was never an aggressive mood. I recall several British golfers who tried to imitate Ouimet's mental approach to the game. All they did was increase their blood pressure and shot-total. They became over-serious, whereas Ouimet was often on the verge of some light-hearted pleasantry. Few men could look back on such a successful playing career, but it was never triumph through gloom. Ouimet had his share of intense concentration, yet remained always companionable. For that reason it was pleasing when, at fifty-eight years of age, he became the first American and the first non-British national to be honoured by election to the Captaincy of the Royal and Ancient Golf Club, an office which had been held by King George VI, the Duke of Windsor and the Duke of Kent. It involved that interesting ceremony performed annually for many generations, the 'driving into office' of the new Captain. The hour is early for all but enthusiasts. Golfers must need be abroad by seven-thirty in the morning if they wish to see all the preliminaries. On that occasion the morning was fair. It was late September at its best, an Indian summer with dew on the grass and waves breaking gently on the beach. Just before eight o'clock Francis Ouimet was escorted to the first tee by a group that included ex-Captains Lord Balfour of Burleigh, Lord Simon, Lord Teviot, Sir George Cunningham, Bernard Darwin, Cyril Tolley and Roger Wethered. The ball was teed by William Auchterlonie, the Club professional and Open Champion of 1893, the year Ouimet was born. The town clock struck the hour. Ouimet drove a confident ball straight down the fairway. The old-fashioned cannon, shifted from the mound behind the clubhouse, was fired with a spluttering roar. Bunched caddies rushed for the ball. The one who retrieved it from the scrimmage was rewarded with a gold American five-dollar piece instead of the former golden sovereign. The ceremony was over. Ouimet had not only played himself into office, he had won automatically the Medal presented to the Club by Queen Adelaide.

It was difficult to know which aspect of his golfing career had merited the honour. As a player, Ouimet's record was impressive. Not only had he won both the Open and Amateur Championships of the United States, but he played against Great Britain in the Walker Cup matches from their inauguration in 1922 until 1936, and afterwards served as non-playing captain. On the other hand, his contributions to the welfare of the game in the role of legislator and administrator were outstanding. Behind-the-scenes contributions have to be off the record. Few golfers realize the volume of administrative detail that has to be tackled by the ruling bodies. Committee work can be tedious, irritating and a waste of time, but not all comes under such headings. After the Second World War ended, British and American golfers played the game under different codes, which could lead to abuse and misunderstanding. I recall a conversation with Ouimet in 1947 in his hotel room at St Andrews. The Walker Cup match had just ended on an harmonious note. Ouimet emphasized that such feeling was of greater value than the actual result of international matches, but much depended on a more unified interpretation of the rules. At that time, there was a difference of opinion about the stymie.

A few years later this gulf had widened with the introduction of new British rules which reduced certain penalties and added various innovations. The danger of taking diverse paths was apparent. In May 1951, action was taken. A United States delegation travelled to this country to confer with Empire representatives. The problems were tackled with imagination. Concessions were made on both sides. Agreement was reached. The draft, with a few modifications, was approved by the United States Golfing Association in July. Finally, it was ratified by St Andrews. The game was governed on both sides of the Atlantic by a unified code. Irregularities ended. The negotiations called for tact, patience and knowledge. In this respect, Francis Ouimet is remembered as one of the main architects in restoring Anglo-American golfing unity.

Abe Mitchell

Abe Mitchell was a golfer whose natural greatness never received its full reward. He bridged two eras. His playing career went back to the heyday of John Ball, Harold Hilton, and Harry Vardon, yet he played in the 1933 Ryder Cup match at Southport and Ainsdale alongside such men as Padgham, Perry, Sarazen and Hagen.

At the outset of his career Mitchell was a prominent member of the Cantelupe Artisan Club at Forest Row. His handicap on the plus-ten mark

Abe Mitchell, whose natural greatness as a golfer never received its full reward. History remembers him as the finest golfer who never won the Open.

indicates his promise. Forest Row expectations were confirmed at Hoylake in 1910 when he was chosen for the England side against Scotland, later reaching the semi-final of the Amateur Championship. In 1912 Mitchell reached the final of the Amateur at Westward Ho – a final that ranks high among the finest of this event. On the run of play he should have won but threw away his chances. Advantage off the tee gave him a three-hole lead over Ball at the end of the first round. He failed to keep up the pressure after lunch and the match was squared on the thirty-third green. The next hole was halved after Ball coped with a partial stymie. Mitchell won the thirty-fifth but missed a short putt that would have given him the match and title. The thirty-seventh was halved. At the thirty-eighth, Mitchell found a ditch and in recovering knocked the ball against his body. That was that. It almost summed up his championship record. Time and again titles might have been his if only the putter had not faltered.

The following year Mitchell took professional status. He finished fourth in the 1914 Open at Prestwick. The war years interrupted a career that should have touched its peak. When championship golf resumed in 1920 at Deal he began as if to make up for lost time. Opening rounds of 74 and 73 gave him a six-shot advantage over Sandy Herd. In the third round fortune reversed. Duncan returned a brilliant 71. Mitchell could do nothing right and returned 84. Duncan went on to card a 72 which was good enough to take the title by two strokes from Herd. Mitchell had to be content with fourth place after a final round of 76. Ted Ray elbowed his way into third place. It is possible that had Mitchell won, his name would have appeared more than once on the trophy. As it is, history ranks him as the greatest player who never won the Open Championship.

Abe was a natural golfer, a long hitter who at times paid the price for exceptional power by excursions in the rough like Severiano Ballesteros. His rhythmic action was copybook. Long irons were not his forte but approach shots were played with unerring accuracy. He mastered the art of rolling two shots into one. He was a strong putter who insisted on giving the hole a chance. His green record was impressive but stopped short of brilliance. My memory of Mitchell is of a strong compact figure, neatly dressed, quiet in mannerisms, with cap well over his eyes, hitting the ball far down the fairway with an abbreviated follow-through. Just as so many good professionals were outpaced in the heyday of the Triumvirate, so it was unfortunate that the latter part of his career coincided with a formidable American invasion.

Abe Mitchell was one of the finest match players Britain has had. There was a magnificence about his game that impressed all who watched. In a quiet, unassuming way he added natural dignity to the title of professional golfer.

William M'Kellar and John Kay

On the links the antics of that enthusiastic golfer William M'Kellar belong to history; his amusing habit of exclaiming whenever he hit a golf ball, 'By the la' Harry this shall not go for nothing'; how, at the suggestion of M'Ewan and Douglas Gourlay, the club- and ball-maker at Bruntsfield, the artist Kay was persuaded to go for a walk on the links, and how, finding the 'Cock o' the Green' engrossed in his usual serious pastime, succeeded in obtaining a characteristic likeness; of M'Kellar's reaction upon being told what had happened, 'What a pity! By gracious had I known, I would have shown him some of my capers.' That print, executed in 1803, is familiar to many golfers, whilst the mutilated copperplate hangs in the Royal Barnton smoking-room.

All that is familiar ground, but not so much is known of the artist. John Kay has been called the only caricaturist that Scotland has produced. It is a debatable point, but what is certain is that his portraits display striking originality. Robert Chambers described them as 'the most exact and faithful likenesses that could have been represented by any mode or art. Kay drew the man as he walked the street every day – his gait, his costume, every peculiarity of his appearance.' Professor Gregory Smith referred to the series of Edinburgh portraits as 'a series unrivalled by any other city'. His claim is justified. I doubt if any other city can produce a similar collection that could equal, let alone surpass, the extent of Kay's *Original Portraits*. They record a faithful picture of one of the most interesting periods in the history of Edinburgh, a time enriched by such men as Scott, Allan Ramsay and Burns. Among Kay's subjects were many who were interested in golf, which is understandable, for of the ten golf clubs said to have been formed in the eighteenth century, Edinburgh and the surrounding district could claim the Royal Burgess Golfing Society, the Honourable Company of Edinburgh Golfers, Bruntsfield Links and the Royal Musselburgh Clubs, all coming into being during the lifetime of the artist. In his *Portraits* it is mentioned that the insignia of the Burgess Golfing Society consisted of an embroidered star worn on the left breast, showing two clubs and two (eventually altered to three) balls, with motto, 'Far and Sure'. It is thought that this insignia and motto formed the Burgess's only coat of arms until the Musselburgh clubhouse was erected in 1875.

As to the man himself, John Kay was born in Dalkeith in 1742. In 1771 he purchased for £40 the freedom of Edinburgh. His occupation was that of a barber-artist, carrying on his trade in a little shop in Parliament Close, but in 1786 he decided to concentrate on art. His earliest etching, bearing the date 1786, is of himself and acts as the frontispiece of the *Original Portraits*. It shows Kay sitting in a high-backed chair. On the back sits his favourite cat, reputed to have been the largest in Scotland. A scroll is in the artist's hand. On his knee is a volume. The table by his side has painting materials and a large bust of Homer. Kay died at 227 High Street, Edinburgh, in 1826, and was buried in the churchyard of Greyfriars Church, leaving in etchings some 900 plates.

Scotland can claim among its early golfers another distinguished artist. In the records of the Honourable Company is a brief entry dated 28 January 1792, signed by James Dalrymple, the Captain: 'Mr Henry Raeburn, formally proposed by Mr William Grant, and seconded by the Captain, was this day ballotted for and admitted,' becoming a member. His description by Scott is detailed. Raeburn was painting himself ... 'I see him in my mind's eye with his hand upon his chin, contemplating his picture; which position always brought me in mind of a figure of Jupiter which I have somewhere seen.' Raeburn made a striking figure, being tall, well made, and usually dressed in voluminous clothes, black leggings and a broad brimmed hat. He was born in a cottage by the Water of Leith at Stockbridge. He was inclined to be quiet, cautious and shrewd, yet there must have been another side to his nature, for on occasions he accompanied David Martin, then a leading Scottish portrait painter and his patron, to Johnnie Dowie's tavern in Liberton's Wynd, a favourite meeting-place of kindred golfing spirits made famous by Burns. The knighthood was conferred on him by George IV at Hopetoun House in August, 1822, just before the King's embarkation. The following year the King appointed Raeburn his 'Limner and Painter in Scotland, with all fees, profits, salaries, rights and privileges, and advantages thereto belonging.'

Then comes the following record preserved in *Golfiana Miscellanea*, dated 1887: 'Sir Henry Raeburn, the great painter, though ardently devoted to the duties of his studio throughout the week, made an exception of Saturday afternoon always in favour of golf. Dr Duncan tells us that on the first Saturday of June, 1823, he played with the ancient artist on Leith

Links what proved to be Sir Henry's last game, the distinguished artist being then in his 80th year.'

Dr Duncan may have been right, but, after that game on Leith, Raeburn visited Fifeshire with Scott, Lord Chief Commissioner Adam and Sir Adam Ferguson. Their tour included St Andrews. I find it difficult to imagine this eminent painter, so keen on the game, being able to resist the Old Course. The day after his return, he complained of feeling unwell, retired to bed and died on 8 July 1823.

6

A Different World

THE PERIOD after the First World War seems light years away. It is difficult to realize how everyday life has changed. When George Duncan was winning the 1920 Open Championship at Deal, police were giving permission for cars to be used in London instead of horses, whilst car-tax was levied at £1 per horsepower. Traffic lights appeared for the first time in Piccadilly. Our current economic problems seem minor compared with the German mark that stood at 4-trillion to the dollar, a loaf of bread in Berlin costing more than 200 billion marks. There was the Wall Street crash and the General Strike, whilst our unemployment exceeded two million. Certain news items had a familiar note. Seventy years ago six policemen were murdered by the IRA, whilst Sinn Fein declared that an arson campaign would make government of Ireland by Britain impossible. Proposals for a Channel Tunnel were rejected by the Government. The Greenhouse Effect seemed anticipated when rain ended a 100-day drought, followed by the worst summer since 1879.

There was no Andrew Lloyd Webber monopoly, but three plays were running in London's West End from the imaginative pen of Edgar Wallace. Petrol soared to 1/1d per gallon. Public vehicles circulated in Hyde Park for the first time since 1836. An American State introduced a bizarre punishment ... motorists who killed a pedestrian had to spend an hour alone with the corpse. Post-war changes were taking shape in the name of progress, bridged by the continuity of golf. Championship venues were the same with names like Hoylake, Prestwick, Muirfield and St Andrews. Amateur golf in the Twenties flourished, dominated by the Triumvirate of Sir Ernest Holderness, Roger Wethered and Cyril Tolley.

Cyril Tolley

The last named was a law unto himself, remembered as one of the great figures in the history of the game. Majestic and dominant, Tolley annihilated distance with a rhythmic swing of aesthetic joy. He combined immense power with a delicate putting touch and established a regal supremacy. Born in September, 1895, Tolley served in the Royal Tank Corps from 1915–19, was taken prisoner and later awarded the Military Cross. He learnt his golf in Eastbourne, but first came into prominence when he went to University College, Oxford, in 1919.

He was persuaded by a fellow undergraduate to enter for the Amateur Championship at Muirfield. Although badly out of practice, he mastered the narrow fairways and reached the final where his opponent was R. A. Gardner, who had won the American Amateur title in 1909 and was a finalist in 1916. Tolley was not overawed and stood 3 up with 4 to play when the American fought back to square the match at the 36th. Both players found the green at the 37th. Gardner laid his ball dead. Tolley lined up the putt, handed his caddie a five-pound note which he had promised in the event of victory, and proceeded to hole-out for 2. Tolley became an international figure with a natural genius for the game. Many successes included a further Amateur title, with perhaps his finest victories being in the French Open Championships of 1924 and 1938. Cyril's preference was 1924. The entry was exceptionally strong, including Gene Sarazen and Walter Hagen. The first two rounds saw him paired with Arnaud Massey, who had tied with Harry Vardon in the 1911 Open Championship. In the fourth round Hagen had a brilliant round of 66. At that time Tolley had six holes to play: carded the first four in par figures: two 5s were needed for victory. At the 450-yard 17th, he was short, but a confident run-up produced a 4. 6 at the last hole would win the title. It is a notoriously difficult hole. Slice meant out-of-bounds, hook could end up behind an orchard. He played safe, took an iron from the tee and finished eighty yards short. A smooth pitch-and-run finished a foot from the pin. Four went on the card. Hagen was beaten by 3 strokes. Tolley rated it his best and most satisfying performance. Four years later he took the title again on the same course with an aggregate of 283, 7 shots better than 1924, this time aided by some prodigious putts.

Tolley's tremendous power was remarkable. In the Jubilee Vase on the Old Course, St Andrews, he twice drove the 18th green on the same day. In the Open Championship at Troon in 1923, he drove the green at the

350-yard first and holed the putt for a 2. He holed-out in one at the 6th at Huntercombe, did the same at the Alps in Hoylake and the 17th at Addington. His longest match was against Bobby Jones at St Andrews in 1930, the American winning at the 19th with a stymie.

Cyril Tolley and Roger Wethered were the greatest golfers ever to come from one University. I go further and nominate Cyril as the most outstanding English amateur after Bobby Jones.

Roger Wethered

Roger Wethered, a thoughtful golfer, played with machine-like precision. If he had a weakness, the driver was the rogue club. J. H. Taylor used to say that had Wethered used irons off the tee, the history of the Walker Cup might have been different. This veteran professional's regard for Wethered was considerable. He rated him as one of the finest amateur iron players of his day with shots of knife-like crispness, but he deplored the tendency to use an iron technique with woods. He was a shrewd judge of golfing skills, but I felt the comments on Roger's Walker Cup record were somewhat at variance with facts. His opponents in five Walker Cup matches were Francis Ouimet, Jesse Sweetser, W. C. Fownes, Jesse Guilford, 'Chick' Evans, Robert Gardner, George von Elm, Johnny Goodman, George Voigt, Bobby Jones and Lawson Little. Against this fearsome galaxy of talent, Wethered had four foursomes victories from five matches plus a half and a win against Ouimet in singles.

The halved match against Ouimet at St Andrews in 1923 was an epic struggle as the American recalled: 'At one hole Roger's shot was at least 40 feet from the cup on a green as fast as lightning. If he could place his putt dead, it seemed he would be accomplishing a miracle. My second left me a ten-footer. Roger putted his trans-continental putt and holed it. The shock was too much for me.' Wethered's putting touch was again a determining factor in the 1923 Amateur final when he beat Robert Harris by 7 and 6, but the magic deserted him in the 1930 Walker Cup match when Bobby Jones crushed him 9 and 8.

The 1921 Open Championship at St Andrews developed into a cut-and-thrust duel between Wethered and 'Jock' Hutchison, the son of a local fisherman, who as a lad had carried clubs on the Old Course. One of his gentlemen was W. C. Carnegie, nephew of the famous Andrew Carnegie. This chance hiring changed his life. With parental consent, Jock went to the United States as private professional to Carnegie, became an American citizen, then professional at the Glen View, Chicago, won the American Professional Match-play title in 1920 and missed out in the United States Open by one stroke.

Wethered far from being overawed by Hutchison's record, was desperately unlucky not to win the title. The result was affected by a penalty stroke at the 14th in the third round. Wethered walked backwards, eyeing the line for the stroke, and accidentally trod on his ball. Had that not happened he would have been two strokes ahead with 18 holes to play. Instead Hutchison's last round of 70 matched by Wethered's fighting finish of 71 gave the American a tie. In the play-off next day the Englishman was beaten by 9 strokes. The breaks had gone Hutchison's way. In the first round he did the 8th in one and just missed repeating the feat at the 9th; consecutive holes with a par of 7 in 3 makes an enormous difference. Moreover, he had critics. His shot-making was undoubtedly helped by ribbed, scorefaced mashies that produced tremendous backspin, an aid later to become barred. The American celebrated victory at the harbour end of St Andrews with fishermen and caddies. Little did we know it marked the beginning of a twelve-year sequence of American successes in the Open, broken only by Arthur Havers' lone victory in 1923. The 1921 Open marked the debut of Bobby Jones in this event. He preferred to forget it. A wayward outward half of 46, followed by 6 at the 10th, and the same figure at the short 11th, made him tear up his card and retire.

Nothing can detract from Roger Wethered's outstanding record. His term of office as Captain of the Royal and Ancient Golf Club added fresh dignity to his memory.

Sir Ernest Holderness

The third member of this Triumvirate was Sir Ernest Holderness, quite different in temperament, adopting an icy detachment with exceptional powers of concentration. He lacked the physical impact of Tolley. Not for him the flamboyant flourish, but he compensated with accurate shot-making, particularly with irons and smooth greenwork. Confident match-player, he won the President's Putter at Rye for several years running. At Prestwick in 1922, he met W. I. Hunter in the semi-final of the Amateur Championship, then holder of the title, and looking to be a repeat champion. At the 15th, Hunter stood 1 up, needed a 3-foot putt to win the hole and became 2 up with 3 to play. Overconfidence proved costly. An over-strong putt left a stymie, and the hole was lost, all square.

Holderness seized the chance and won the match. The next day he defeated a Scot, John Caven, by 1 up.

In 1924 Holderness again reached the Amateur Championship final at St Andrews. It lacked international flavour. A final between two Englishmen can be a hard sell to a Scottish gallery, but neutrality is quickly forgotten when the quality of golf is high. His opponent was Eustace Storey. Cambridge University captain and in his fourth year as a student, he played well but could not subdue Holderness who coped with heavy rain and wind. The margin was 3 and 2.

Out of the first five Amateur Championships after the war, the Triumvirate had won four: Cyril Tolley in 1920, Roger Wethered in 1923, and Sir Ernest Holderness in 1922 and 1924. Technically Holderness was a weekend golfer who worked five days a week as a Civil Servant. He was a genuine Amateur Champion.

In 1921 the Open Championship went to the United States for the first time. The manner in which 'Jock' Hutchison won the title I have already described in the study of Roger Wethered. Little did we think that with one exception the trophy was to cross the Atlantic for the next twelve years. The monopoly was humiliating. Confidence was eroded. Only occasionally was their cause for self-congratulating relief. On this short list was a professional rough-hewn out of granite. I refer to Ted Ray.

Ted Ray

A prodigious smiter, tall and powerfully built, Ray took no half measures. He put every ounce of his considerable weight into the stroke, but a distinct forward lunge of the body often invited wayward shots. Cartoonists used to show him hacking his way out of a forest of bents and whins. His style was cobbled, but had definite rhythm in the swing. His recipe is remembered in an oft-quoted answer to one of his pupils who was trying to get more length to his drives: 'Hit it a bloody sight harder, mate.' Those who can look back over many years of championship golf will remember Ray walking across the fairways with hat carelessly placed on the back of his head, puffing clouds of smoke from his favourite pipe. He looked so delightfully casual, and this happy-go-lucky streak seemed on the surface to run through his game as he wielded his niblick in the rough. Appearances were deceptive. Ted Ray was a formidable golfer whose skill is available for posterity in the records. His robust humour came to the fore when he described the early years of his life. Born in 1877, he claimed he swung a club as soon as he could walk. The first one was made by his father. The head was one of the wooden pins used by fishermen for mending nets. With the help of a red-hot poker, a hole was made into which was fitted a thorn stick and the club was complete. Ray called it the first of the socket type of club. The next stage was fashioning his own clubs with a pocket knife from any suitable wood he found in the lanes. His juvenile career ended when he became the owner of a real golf club. He used to compare his golf beginnings with those of Sandy Herd, who adapted shinty sticks cut from Strathtyrum Woods, using champagne corks, found on a refuse heap behind the Royal and Ancient Golf Club, as golf balls, weight being added by inserting screw-nails into the corks. Ray said he would have liked to play Sandy Herd and Laurie Auchterlonie on their childhood links of the cobblestoned streets of St Andrews, with lampposts for flags at the cathedral end of North Street. The daydreams of all three boys came true in the Open Championships of America and this country.

Ted Ray was a giant personality in every sense of the word. His style was individualistic to a remarkable degree: essentially a natural player, the artistic side of his game was overshadowed by the efficiency of his methods. His long driving and powers of recovery became legendary. He won the 1912 Open Championship at Muirfield. Of all his many triumphs, I isolate an incredible last round in the 1920 American Open Championship at Inverness, Toledo. With 9 holes to play, Harry Vardon led the field by 4 strokes, added another at the 11th, and looked set for victory, then on the 12th tee of the longest hole, a sudden squall of gale-force intensity had to be fought. Length and accuracy became affected. Four shots were needed to reach the green. A stroke was lost, then another at the 13th. The squall died away, but Vardon was a spent force. He lost 6 shots over the last seven holes and finished in a tie with Jack Burke at 296. Ted Ray finished with 295 and took the lead. Then came Jock Hutchison and Leo Diegel with 'Chick' Evans carrying his clubs. Each had a long putt on the last green to tie with Ray. At the 72nd, five men could have won. In the end Vardon, Burke, Hutchison and Diegel tied for second place, one shot behind Ted Ray.

Jim Barnes

The 1925 Open at Prestwick highlighted the difference between championship golf then and now. What happened turned out to be near fiasco. With the absence of the holder, Walter Hagen, and his amateur challenger, Bobby Jones, the title was up for grabs. The pace-makers were two naturalized Americans, Cornish-born Jim Barnes and the Scottish-claimed Macdonald Smith. Drama boiled over on the final day.

MacSmith had carded an indifferent first round of 76 against a record 70 by Barnes, but in the next round counter-attacked with a new record of 69 to take a two-stroke lead. The draw for the final two rounds made Smith a late starter with Barnes drawing an 8 a.m. slot. When Barnes drove off he faltered, failed to get his act together and returned 79. Smith's 76 increased his lead to five. Barnes was fortunate in the final round. Crowds of spectators had yet to arrive by train from Glasgow. Soon they were milling around the fairways excited at the prospect of a semi-Scottish victory. Their mood became uncontrolled, particularly at the 3rd, the Cardinal, where play was held up by swarming crowds. These delays broke Macdonald Smith's concentration. His drive found trouble. Six went on the card. Every hole thereafter became a nightmare of confusion. Forty-two to the turn left 36 needed to tie with Barnes who was already in the clubhouse with an aggregate of 301. Eventually MacSmith completed the round in 82, finishing fourth behind Ted Ray, Archie Compston and Barnes. MacSmith was bitter and blamed the crowd for the collapse. The ironic twist was that all these spectators were wanting him to win. There were just too many of them on a links ill-adapted for even rudimentary crowd control. The incidents led to gate-money being introduced by the Royal and Ancient Club in 1926, the admission charge being 2/6d. The cost was considered excessive.

Jim Barnes was the only Cornishman to win both British and American Open titles. He was also the tallest, and probably the thinnest, champion in the record books. I mention these two facts because a tall, thin man is generally at a disadvantage when it comes to shot-making. Barnes overcame the physical handicap by taking a widish stance, legs taut, keeping well down throughout the shot. There was no suggestion of the usual tendency to rise too soon. His clubs were on the short side. He putted with a cleek and used a wide stance on the greens. In 1955 Barnes paid a visit to this country from America where he had settled. We met in Lytham during the Amateur Championship and talked about Lelant. He was looking forward to returning to his birthplace, his fear being that it might be completely changed. I assured him that Cornwall is one of the few places in Britain that never seemed to change. In Lelant he would find that the sand dunes still crept up to the village. In the church the slate monument of William Praed still knelt with his wife and four children, the wife wearing the wide-brimmed, high-crowned hat. The eighteenth-century sundial with a figure holding an hourglass is still in a niche over the porch. And in the clubhouse the visitor today will find that the memory and deeds of Jim Barnes are still kept fresh, whilst the Secretary is custodian of most interesting memorabilia. The years are pushed back.

Arthur Havers

When Arthur Havers died in 1981, he was at eighty-two the oldest surviving Open Champion. He won the title in 1923 when the event was held at Troon for the first time. His consistency was enough to withstand the American challenge: three 73s and a final round of 76 kept Walter Hagen in second place by a single shot. He did not repeat the success. In the third round of the 1932 Open at Prince's, his 68 put him in contention, only to fall away in the final round. In that light he was a puzzle. Endowed with a splendid physique, controlled style and placid temperament, he seemed unable to rouse himself for a final effort. After Troon, ambition did not burn so fiercely. His match-play record was impressive. In 1924 he visited America and beat Bobby Jones, then American champion, by 2 and 1 over 36 holes, and Gene Sarazen by 5 and 4 over 72 holes. The unofficial match against America in 1926 saw him defeat McLeod by 10 and 9. In the Ryder Cup matches of 1927, 1931 and 1933 he won singles against Leo Diegel and Craig Wood.

Havers' approach to golf was that of a master craftsman. In appearance and ability he stood head and shoulders above most of his colleagues. He had about his bearing an air of courtesy and dignity. Never ruffled, outwardly imperturbable, he paced life to suit his mental tempo. His attributes made him uncontroversial; his undoubted popularity was helped through having few axes to grind. In all discussions he gave patient, thoughtful observations. An honorary member of the Royal and Ancient Club, Arthur Gladstone Havers was a credit to his profession.

Walter Hagen

I now come to a remarkable man, Walter Hagen, prototype of a new generation of professionals, difficult, if not impossible, to categorize. He was different in every sense of the word. Alongside homespun colleagues, Hagen stood out as a sartorial fashion-plate; well-cut suits, ready eye for feminine charm, unquestionably vain, at times he would change his entire outfit between rounds on the same day. Hagen enjoyed life. Many of his brittle observations have survived. 'I don't want to die a millionaire, just to live like one.' When he died at Traverse City, Michigan, at the age of seventy-six, that wish had been realized, for whilst he was the first professional to make a million, the money was spent just as quickly. One extravagence was a passion for luxury cars, pride and joy being his open tourer Sturtz Bearcat, one of the most expensive automobiles of his day. In this country he settled for a rented Rolls-Royce. He hated to go to bed, arguing that it seemed stupid to spend half of one's life unconscious. Personal philosophy never varied. Making money was important, but pointless unless there was time to pause and smell the flowers as he made his way through life.

So much for personal idiosyncrasies. His impact on the game anticipated the influence exercised seventy years later by the likes of Arnold Palmer and Jack Nicklaus. Hagen was that far ahead of his time. He won two United States Open Championships, four Open Championships, plus five American Professional Championships, four in succession, a remarkable sequence that included twenty-two consecutive wins over 36 holes against the finest professionals. He had a rare ability to forget failures. Over 72 holes against Archie Compston at Moor Park in 1928, he lost a challenge match by 18 and 17 for £500. A week later he won the Open Championship. In a return challenge match at Westchester Club, he reversed the result. George Duncan had a similar purple when he beat Hagen 10 and 8 in the 1929 Ryder Cup match at Moortown, but the American won his third Open at Sandwich the same season. Three years later he partnered Densmore Shute and trounced Duncan and Havers by 10 and 9. In all Hagen made five Ryder Cup appearances and was made captain in 1937. His first Open was a flop, He finished 46th. The following week he won the French Open title. He travelled the world with Joe Kirkwood, often giving a remarkable trick show, then did a similar trip with Horton Smith, the American boywonder whose career was regrettably affected by a broken wrist in a car crash. During that 1928–9 tour Hagen won seven of the first eleven tournaments.

Arthur Havers, the benign 1923 Open
Champion, listens with arms folded to the Mayor
of Southampton stressing a non-golfing point.
Haver's solitary win was a landmark in that it
stemmed the all-conquering Americans.

Walter Hagen ... much of the American
supremacy in championship golf was due to the
example set by this player. He was the first of the
giants of machine-like precision.

The Haig exuded good-humour. Nothing unsettled him, even at a prize-giving when a law officer claimed the cheque for alimony. Temperamentally, he was ideally equipped for the big occasion. Others were more skilful, but when the chips were down and stake-money good, his self-confidence unnerved many an opponent. His gamesmanship was worthy of W. G. Grace's wile. It never paid to underestimate him. He would saunter through a key match with apparent casual indifference that was deceptive. Such insouciance was a shrewd veneer. In a split second the frivolous cloak disappeared. In its place came ice-cold concentration. Hagen was the Jekyll and Hyde of the links. Superficially he was a bundle of contradictions, a walking paradox, but there was nothing untidy or slovenly about his make-up. He was a calculating strategist. He analysed his opponent, noted a possible weakness then concentrated upon it like a boxer switching his attack on a defensive flaw.

This was confirmed by Bobby Jones. He described a match in which his drives were leaving Hagen miles behind. To outdrive Hagen was unusual, for in previous meetings the professional had invariably been stronger off the tee. After a few holes Jones noticed that Hagen was driving with his brassy and gave the reason that he was not on speaking terms with his driver. Jones thought differently. He believed that Hagen was confident that his iron play was superior. By playing short he was able to emphasize the difference. Psychologically Hagen was right. Few things are more discouraging in a match than to see your opponent sight the pin with every iron and then be called to go one better.

Stories about Hagen are legion. The following one reflects something of his calculating approach. It occurred at Brae Burn in 1919 when he tied with Mike Brady for the United States Open. At the 17th in the play-off, Hagen sliced into the rough, the ball finishing on soft ground. The ball was trodden on by the gallery, becoming inbedded in the mud. The official in charge ruled that it should be played as it was, for no one was certain that it had been stepped on. Hagen protested but the ruling had been given. The next thing was to bypass the decision. He asked to identify the ball. The point was conceded. The official turned the ball over a number of times. Hagen was still not convinced. By the time most of the mud had been removed the soil around was loose. The ball was once more playable, a ploy that possibly saved three shots.

As a player Hagen's putting was impressive. He used a blade putter with a rather flat lie, and with a velvety touch would address the ball opposite his left toe. Before the wedge appeared, he developed an uncanny knack of getting down in 2 from near-impossible lies, strokes inspired by sheer artistry. Woods were the least impressive shots in his armoury. Every round had one or two crooked drives. Long iron shots were excellent; bunker shots immaculate. Knee action was suspect. He was not a smooth free swinger. On the other hand, a radical change might have upset a style that won every major title. Only in the closing years of his career was he ever without a golf title. Other golfers were more mechanical and less prone to error, but none had a temperament more suited to the big occasion. The name of Walter Hagen is solidly entrenched in the history of the game, one of its greatest competitors and shrewdest showman of the links.

7

W. T. Linskill – the Eternal Student

EVERY sport has a quota of individuals whose conduct, utterances and foibles have the makings of legends. Golf is no exception. I pick out W. T. Linskill, a rare personality who was fascinated by ghost stories, regretted he had never seen one, was a self-appointed custodian of the Old Course, St Andrews, and delighted in claiming that he introduced golf to Cambridge. He was the son of Captain Linskill, Mayor of Tyneside, and the Hon. Mrs Linskill, was educated at Jesus College, Cambridge, and made first contact with golf on holidays with his parents, becoming an enthusiast with Young Tom Morris as his tutor. He was elected a member of the Royal and Ancient Golf Club in 1875.

Linskill's claim to have introduced the game to Cambridge was perhaps slightly exaggerated, though unquestionably his enthusiasm led to the inauguration of the match between Oxford and Cambridge Universities. Keenness was certainly needed to justify the early start for these matches, the wearisome journey to London, the drive to Waterloo, train to Putney, another conveyance to the London Scottish Iron Hut, well-earned lunch, and eventually a round of golf to decide the issue for a year. As regards the beginning of golf in Cambridge, this is what Linskill himself had to say on the subject:

'It was in 1873 when I first started the game at Coe Fen and Sheep's Green amid much derision and chaff. I taught one or two chaps to play and finally we discovered Coldham Common and started a club there. I cut the holes, rolled the greens, marked the tees and minded clubs, also acted as teacher. No one knew this Scottish game and nearly everyone despised it.' He failed to record that this Coldham Common course had abominable lies through the green and a poisonous smell from an adjoining glue-works which at times made the playing of the far holes almost impossible. This claim was questioned by Lord Dunedin when addressing the Committee of the Cambridge University Golf Club in King's College. He questioned Linskill's statement,

It seemed to me impossible that in 1873 the only people who knew golf in Cambridge were people who were taught by Linskill. There must have been Scotch boys who had surely played golf at home, for I well remember a former generation, even a generation in front of me, who, although they did not play golf at Cambridge, had played it in Scotland. One of my predecessors was William Muir, who won, very shortly afterwards, the St. Andrews Medal. I do not want to take away from Mr Linskill the great credit to which he is entitled. I think he was the founder of your club, and certainly he was the first person who brought off university matches, but I do not think he was the founder of golf at Cambridge.

Lord Dunedin added personal reminiscences:

I learned golf first in 1866. It was quite true that I had a golf club long before that. I was given a golf club by a tutor. He taught me to play in the beginning of June 1857. I was in Perthshire at the time and an inland links was utterly unknown. It was supposed that you could only play golf by the sea-shore or on the banks of a river, so I only began golf in Edinburgh during my holidays from Harrow at Musselburgh in 1866. When I became eighteen in 1868 I was elected a member of the Honourable Company of Edinburgh Golfers. I came up to Cambridge for my first term in October 1868. I cannot remember if I brought my clubs with me in 1868, but I certainly did in 1869 and I went out and practised by myself on Midsummer Common.

Towards the close of the forties the parson at Northam Burrows in Devonshire, not far from Bideford, was a certain Mr Gosset. His sister married one of the Moncrieffs of St. Andrews. Gosset went up there to visit his brother-in-law and his new relations taught him golf. Being a sensible man, he considered that there was a place where golf could be played near his own home and they began to play golf in a desultory sort of way at Northam Burrows, which ended finally with the Westward Ho Club being founded in 1864. Gosset had a son, George, who was at King's at the same time as I was. He had also thought about golf and he started playing on Midsummer Common with another King's man. It came to the knowledge of us two and we made friends upon the strength of it. We put our heads together and came to the conclusion that Midsummer Common was no use. In the first place it was a place where you really could not have a links; secondly, you could get into frightful trouble for hitting people; so, wondering where we could go, we thought we would go and prospect at Royston.

Their methods were primitive, as all beginnings are in golf, be it Fife or Hertfordshire.

Gosset and I went over to Royston one day accompanied by two bags of clubs and a hole-cutter which he had brought from Westward Ho. In Royston we picked up three little boys and went to the heath. Surveying the land, we started, and decided here should be the eighteenth hole and the tee shall be there. We settled that the first hole should be a long one and we looked with our eye and fixed the spot where the hole should be. We hit two full shots and then we played the approach shot. Then we cut the hole – and remember the hole was not cut in the way of making an isosceles triangle of which the base was the line between our two balls – it was honestly kept where we said it would be, and we did the putting. We went through the eighteeen holes like that, and I really believe that is probably a unique round of golf. When we returned we spoke to our friends and inserted an advertisement in the paper.

Claude Carnegie, a Scotsman who lived in Forfar, added a footnote. He wrote to Lord Dunedin,

I have no record of the club but what really happened was this – that in response to an advertisement seventeen of us turned up, including Gosset, you and myself. Gosset was elected captain, I was appointed honorary secretary and I took the names and 2s.6d. from everybody. So far as I remember this was in 1869. The end of the term came soon after and the following term I could not get them together again. Some went down, some said Royston was too far off, many never answered my letters, so I was left to only five or six faithfuls.

Lord Dunedin concluded, 'By the end of 1871 everybody went down and nothing more happened. There was some contemporary knowledge of this because there was a letter on 13 November 1869 to *The Field* stating that a club had been formed and describing a match between Gosset and another King's man against myself, playing one ball.'

This evidence would seem to suggest that W. T. Linskill was the inaugurator of the University Match, but credit for founding the first golf club and introducing the game to Cambridge should go to Lord Dunedin, though I am sure golf must have been played in and around Cambridge much earlier than 1869. It had been played in Scotland for over a century and it is unlikely that Scottish youths left their clubs at home when they crossed the Border. Cambridge University records the progress of Linskill in every University Match. In the first contest on a windswept Wimbledon Common in March 1878, he failed to win a single hole against W. S. W. Wilson of Exeter. Oxford, under the captaincy of Horace Hutchinson, who was to become Amateur Champion eight years later, ended the day victors by 24 holes to nil. The following year Cambridge had revenge by 12–2, but Linskill lost by one hole to Andy Stuart, in spite of sinking long putts with his wooden putter which he wielded so effectively in later years. In 1882 Linskill, still captain of the CUGC, failed against Ludovic Grant of Balliol, but the Light Blues won 8–7. Finally in 1883 he ignored the Four Years' Rule and again turned out for Cambridge. This time he halved with Grant, but Oxford gained the day by 15–13. So ended Linskill's reign as Tchekhov's eternal student in favour of a more mature role in St Andrews.

His interests as Dean of Guild were numerous. Inspired by visits to the catacombs of Rome, he was convinced that an underground passage existed between St Andrews cathedral and the castle, which to his delight seemed confirmed after a subterranean passage was discovered when a cottage near the castle was demolished in 1879. Not so successful were his delvings into the supernatural, as he tried to trace records of hauntings amid the ruins of St Andrews. Many of these stories he committed to paper. The effect tended to be somewhat flowery, hardly on a par with *Tales of the Unexpected* on television, but they never lacked imagination. For twenty-five years he contributed in more practical fashion on the St Andrews Town Council. In private he never tired of relating how he escaped death on the train that plunged from the Tay Bridge in December 1879. He was travelling from Edinburgh to St Andrews with the usual change at Leuchars, where a cab was expected to be waiting. Delayed by the stormy conditions, Linskill decided to continue by train to Dundee. Just as he was about to leave a porter called out that the cab had arrived. Linskill and a friend who was travelling with him jumped out of the train as it began to move. Both lives were saved by seconds.

Much about Linskill has a Pickwickian touch. In red coat he used to drive from King's cross to Wimbledon Common in a four-in-hand coach complete with guard and post-horn. His recollections of the Old Course went back to the time of reclamation work on the edge of the first fairways, and were recorded in an article in *Chamber's Journal*:

... between the Royal and Ancient Golf Club and the burn at the first hole, many acres of land have been reclaimed from the German Ocean. Where I can remember the sea-shore once existed, there are now excellent lies for the players' balls. There are, I believe, three sea-walls buried under the golf green, and the old bathing-place was once under the present window of the north room of the Club. The historic Swilcan Burn formerly swept almost into the centre of the Links before it turned into the sea, and one often drove into this bed from the first tee. It was then a sandy natural hazard, but now it is a concrete-walled channel.

Not all was research into architectural and supernatural mysteries. He knew how to enjoy himself. In company with Young Tom Morris and others like-minded, he used to play moonlight matches. The routine was two rounds with dinner in-between, on the Ladies' Putting Course, with candles placed in the holes, a formal version of an impromptu match late at night before a Walker Cup Match and doubtless equally lighthearted. W. T. Linskill died on 22 November 1929, ages seventy-four. He left behind the memory of a portly figure, familiar high collar, high spats and drooping moustache, deceptively pugnacious, for at heart he was a gentle character with a weakness for romantic legends and a passion for golf.

8

The Theories of Macdonald and Simpson

ALONGSIDE these descriptions of how golf courses were originally laid out in primitive fashion, it is interesting to recall how the National Links of America owes its existence to the imagination of Charles B. Macdonald, the controversial, brilliant golf course architect who became obsessed with the dream of designing a course that embodied features of the finest holes in the game. He played over our leading British links, made copious notes, bought 250 acres of land on the shore of Peconic Bay in eastern Long Island and produced the first golfing transplant.

The holes he copied from Britain included the old short par 4 third at Royal St George's; the Alps at Prestwick with its blind second shot over a strategically sited hill and penal bunker; the famous Redan from North Berwick, again with wickedly penalizing bunkering; the Road Hole at St Andrews with traps taking the place of the traditional railway sheds and the notorious bunker by the green. The thirteenth at National was inspired by the Old Course eleventh. A pond introduced a new note but the architect confirmed the source of inspiration by naming the hole after the Eden. The completed course fell short of his original intention. It was an inland test rather than a links course but the concept was novel and exciting.

Tom Simpson was our answer to Charles Macdonald. This doyen of golf course archiects, who died in 1967 at the age of sixty-seven, was a remarkable personality with many facets, unconventional, controversial, individualist, hostile to committees, at times provocative with revolutionary ideas, but many of his observations made sense. He maintained that 'the vital thing about a hole is that it should either be more difficult than it looks or look more difficult than it is. It must never be what it looks.' Sort that out. He further argued that classic principles of design were based on the principles embodied in the greatest of the classics, the Old Course at St Andrews. Ballybunion, Baltray, Monfontaine and Royal Antwerp are but four of the courses that reflected his designing skills. Simpson maintained that a bunker should never be sited to trap a bad shot. If the course had been laid out properly the mistake would find its own punishment. He maintained that most courses were over-bunkered. Redesigning a course in Scotland, he whittled down some 1,300 bunkers to 65. Hoylake and the Old Course represented for him some of the finest examples of true golf course architecture. Tom Simpson, whom I knew for many years, was a rare individual, a connoisseur of golfing excellence and a meticulous purist.

An Eclectic Lay-out

One evening Simpson challenged me to select an eclectic course drawn from the finest holes in the British Isles. It sounded easy, but I had difficulty in weeding out the choice of par threes and the fine array of finishing holes. There are so many magnificent tests. Moreover the yardage had to be balanced. An eclectic lay-out produces many a headache.

1 Hoylake, 420 yards. Par four.
   The round begins with a superb opening hole, dog-legged to the right, flanked by the out-of-bounds cop, about three feet high, that marks the practice ground. The drive should finish past the corner but any hint of a slice is penalized. It can be an unnerving start to the round and a worrying ordeal as a nineteenth or thirty-seventh replay.

2 Birkdale, 427 yards. Par four.
   The second lies in the range of sandhills on the Lancashire coast at Birkdale where the hole winds its way along a valley that bisects the dunes. The prevailing wind makes it an exacting test. The green may be slightly over-defined but the bunkers are craftily sited against a background of dwarf pines. A thoughtful examination of golfing skills.

3 Carnoustie, 384 yards. Par four.
   A testing hole that calls for precision driving and an accurate pitch

over Jockies Burn to a small target green. It looks deceptively straightforward but can be expensive.

4 Turnberry, 170 yards. Par three.
The first short hole takes us to the Mull of Kintyre against a background of Arran mountains. Turnberry was mutilated in the last war but Mackenzie Ross performed an architectural miracle. The fourth, appropriately named Woe-be-Tide, demands pin-point accuracy from the tee. The slightest touch of a hook deposits the ball on the beach.

5 Newcastle, Co Down, 446 yards. Par four.
The setting for the fifth is equally impressive. Royal County Down is laid out beside the mountains and the ocean. Slieve Donard, highest of the Mourne Mountains, makes a backdrop with the Ballynahinch Mountains in the north and the wide expanse of Dundrum Sands. The tee-shot at this right-handed dog-leg has to clear an expanse of heather often in the teeth of the prevailing wind. A firm second is needed to find a well-guarded green in the dunes.

6 Carnoustie, 565 yards. Par five.
Every hole at Carnoustie sets a problem. The sixth is no exception. Under certain conditions it is one of the toughest on the championship rota and has ruined many title hopes. In summer with fast fairways, modern technique ignores the out-of-bounds fence that stretches along the left. Jockies Burn ceases to be troublesome but when the winds sweep across the course, and it is usually windy from the Firth of Tay, the test becomes one of strength and nerve. The bunker at the back of the green takes care of the over-impetuous. Top players can find the hole vicious under such conditions; the average golfer thinks of purgatory.

7 Hoylake, 193 yards. Par three.
No hesitation about this choice. Dowie is one of the finest short holes in the British Isles. The long, slender green is flanked on the left by a crop and out-of-bounds. The opening to the green is marked by a clump of wild rushes. To sight the pin is asking for trouble. An over-strong tee-shot dead on target can end up a few yards away and out of bounds. John Graham used to play it in copybook fashion. He had just enough draw to roll up to the pin. It looks simple, as many imitators have found to their cost.

8 Royal Lytham and St Annes, 394 yards. Par four.
First-class hole laid out in a natural, unspoilt part of the course. It required pin-point accuracy from the tee-shot off a pulpit tee. Veer off line and trouble looms. The approach to the high plateau green must be placed. Bunkers guarding the entrance to the green trap the weak shot. Anything over-strong finishes down the slope at the back. To get par requires intelligent shot-making.

9 Turnberry, 475 yards. Par four.
View from the tee is awe-inspiring. The drive is played from a rocky pinnacle high above the rocks and across a chasm with waves waiting below to a green by Turnberry lighthouse. The length of the tee-shot presents no problem: what tightens the muscles is the thought of the obvious fate if the ball is mishit. Assuming the ball reaches the safety of the fairway, troubles are by no means over. The hog's-back surface can play havoc with second shots. A memorable hole.

10 Muirfield, 475 yards. Par four.
Another first-class hole. Prevailing wind blows across at right angles. Cross-bunkers add to the difficulties of an exacting par four.

11 St Andrews, 170 yards. Par three.
Here is a hole that divides the critics. Tom Simpson dismissed it as one of the worst holes on the Old Course. Others rank it among the finest of short holes. To get par is a relief. Two entrants in the Amateur Championship were thankful to settle for a half in eighteen. Gene Sarazen recalled he once needed six shots. One competitor in a major championship used up 27 shots. The hole is so disarming. It looks so close, so tantalizingly easy, but the green is on an acute slope with Strath bunker on the right and Cockle bunker a little to the right in front of the green. If the teeshot stops above the hole trouble threatens. Let the wind blow in from the Eden and three putts are likely, if not a visit to Hell bunker. An over-strong teeshot could finish in the Eden or rough that makes a down-slope recovery more than chancy. Three on a card is a bonus.

12 Troon, 432 yards. Par four.
A thoughtful hole that changes its character with every variation of wind. It refuses to be taken for granted. Accurate club judgment vital. A hole that encourages artistry in shot-making.

ABOVE Clubhouse of the Royal Lytham and St Anne's Golf Club. Many titles have been decided on the home green.

BELOW The Honourable Company of Edinburgh Golfers at Muirfield claimed by historians and confirmed by historical documents as the oldest Golf Club in the world.

13 Sandwich, 444 yards. Par four.
An outstanding two-shotter curving to the left. Crux comes with the second shot. The entrance to the green looks horribly narrow while strategically placed bunkers are a contributory worry. Even on the green, which slopes slightly, it takes a touch of confidence to read the putt correctly.

14 St Andrews, 560 yards. Par five.
The Long Hole is in a class of its own. It proves that wind is the ultimate hazard. The first thing is to reach the safety of the Elysian Fields after avoiding the out-of-bounds and the Beardies. The next decision is critical. If Hell Bunker can be carried, all is well: that leaves Ginger Beer and Grave bunkers. Even the green is fraught with problems. Its abrupt sloping plateau requires confident, accurate reading.

15 Portmarnock, 192 yards. Par three.
Another short hole of merit. It needs a wind blowing from the sea to impose its punishing qualities. The teeshot is played from a tee up in the sandhills. With the breeze coming from that quarter, it pays to use it by drawing the arc from the beach. Timing must be perfect, otherwise out-of-bounds. Green guarded by two bunkers. Par three has to be earned.

16 Royal Porthcawl, 440 yards. Par four.
Provided the drive finds the fairway sandwiched between sandhills on the right and a fence on the left, the second shot, gauged correctly, should find the green. No alibi if the shot is weak for cross-bunkers are waiting. The plateau green looks innocent but many a shot misses the target. Par four can easily become a six.

17 Road Hole, St Andrews, 446 yards. Par four.
Hole known all over the world: dreaded, respected, almost legendary, graveyard of many championship hopes. No golfer can take liberties with its hazards. There have been changes but its essential character remains. The old railway sheds have gone, instead the drive has to clear part of the hotel grounds. The shot should not present undue difficulties, but if it finds trouble, then heaven help the player when he tackles the second shot. The narrow plateau green is roughly two feet above the fairway: beyond is the road itself waiting for the over-strong ball to roll down the slope. Eating into the front of the green

on the left is the Road bunker. An under-powered second shot that fails to reach the upper level of the narrow-waisted green will see the ball trickle back into the bunker. Recovery from the road is difficult. The landing area is so small with the lay-out drawing into the trap. Undulations on the green require confident reading. Many famous golfers have recorded double figures.

18 Carnoustie, 448 yards. Par four.
This hole was stretched to 525 yards for the Open Championship, but the reduced yardage highlights the influence of the Barry Burn. This water hazard dominates play. From the tee it is in front and on either side with an out-of-bounds fence on the left. When the hole is lengthened there is a tendency to play safe and short, whereas when the carry is attempted on the 448-yard lay-out, the penalty is dire. The burn is some 25 feet wide where it guards the green and there is still the out-of-bounds fence to remember. This hole is worthy to finish an eclectic round of near-architectural perfection. Obviously it would not be everybody's taste. The permutation of alternatives is considerable, but it is not as easy as it seems if balance is to be preserved. Try substituting alongside this layout:

Hole		Yards	Par
1	Hoylake	420	4
2	Birkdale	427	4
3	Carnoustie	384	4
4	Turnberry	170	3
5	Newcastle, Co. Down	446	4
6	Carnoustie	565	5
7	Hoylake	193	3
8	Royal Lytham & St Annes	394	4
9	Turnberry	475	4
10	Muirfield	475	4
11	Old Course, St Andrews	170	3
12	Troon	432	4
13	Sandwich	444	4
14	Old Course, St Andrews	560	5
15	Portmarnock	192	3
16	Porthcawl	440	4

| 17 Old Course, St Andrews | 466 | 4 |
| 18 Carnoustie | 448 | 4 |

Out: 3,474 yards.   par 35
In: 3,627 yards.   par 35
Total: 7,101 yards.   par 70

9

Mirage of the Thirties

LOOKING back, the Thirties seem like a mirage. It was a different world in so many ways, one that the present generation finds hard to appreciate. By today's standards, values were unbelievable. A few examples from the domestic front emphasize the point. Thomas Cook advertised eight days on the French Riviera for £8.17.6. For the more adventurous, first-class return sea-passage on the Orient Line to Australia cost £124, third-class was £57. Food was plentiful and within the reach of every pocket, with eggs one shilling a dozen, butter one shilling per pound, and tea ten pence a pound. A living wage was estimated at £3 a week, with luxury level at £10 a week. The new 14.9 hp Morris Major came on the market at £215.

Golf was similarly different. We still play for the same trophies and titles that were at stake then, but the tempo and style were in a distinctive mould. A more gentlemanly atmosphere had little in common with the current cash-nexus. Team selection for international events was not decided by stake-money success from inflated prize cheques. No doubt progress has been made, but it is alien to the Thirties pattern. Equipment has improved, but basically playing standards are no higher. That decade produced an exceptional rich crop of outstanding golfers with at least two memorable international matches. Memories of those years are identified with hours that have been and can never be again. It is a latent yearning to go back to the spaciousness of one's youth and reconstruct the emotions of an hour. Sadly the years cannot be put back but many of the personalities involved more than qualify for inclusion in the survey of charismatic landmarks in golf history.

The Whitcombe Trinity

This period belongs to the Whitcombes, a remarkable trinity of brothers who between them won every golfing honour this country offers. For almost twenty years they strove to win the Open Championship, only to see victory snatched away. A few results emphasize this point. In 1924 Ernest finished second, Charles was fourth in 1932, fifth in 1922, 1927 and 1934, and third in 1935. Reginald came fifth in 1933, second in 1937. I thought that Carnoustie 1937 might be Reginald's year. The full strength of the American Ryder Cup team was in the field, riding the crest of the wave after beating Great Britain at Southport. The course was exacting, the weather frightful, a combination that played havoc with all but the most powerful shot-makers. Reginald set a cracking pace. The Americans were jolted out of their stride trying to cope with golf as it was intended to be played. Moral victory was Whitcombe's, but final honours were taken by Henry Cotton. The Whitcombes seemed fated. Opportunity rarely knocks twice, but this time pessimists were wrong. The following season the Open went to Sandwich. Again the weather was shocking. Gale-force winds swept across the exposed Royal St George's fairways, where towering sandhills dwarf the player as he makes his way along a dell-like setting. It feels like isolation. There is a remoteness about golf at Sandwich that is unique, an experience never to be forgotten. In a gale only the truly great can hope to succeed on these fairways. On the first two days of the 1938 championship, the going was good and scores were low. On the final day a gale restored the balance. Before a ball was struck, the huge marquee that housed the traders' exhibition was torn to shreds, the contents of the stands scattered everywhere. Scores rocketed. The best was Cotton with 74. At the end only three players managed to break the 300-mark. Rugged players like Jimmy Adams, Alfred Padgham and Reginald were in their element. By chance Whitcombe and Adams were coupled together – entirely different styles. Whitcombe used a short swing; the Scotsman relied on a full swing reminiscent of the old St Andrews swing. Shot for shot they fought it out. As a demonstration how to play shots into the teeth of a gale, the performance of both men was superb. It was wretched luck that once again Adams had to be the runner-up, but it was justice that the Whitcombe name should at last be on the trophy. In one sense it was a shared honour. Between them three eras were bridged. Ernest and Charles saw the close of the Vardon-Taylor-Braid-Herd period, and in company with George Duncan and Abe Mitchell were

Charles Whitcombe had a long and distinguished career. He lacked the rugged personality of Reginald but could look back on a tournament career packed with achievement.

Reginald Whitcombe came close for some twenty years to winning the Open. His moment finally came in 1938 when he won the title at Sandwich in appalling weather and gale-force winds that tore down the huge marquee.

involved in the beginnings of Anglo-American golf rivalry. All three were natural golfers. They grew up on a golf course and almost cut their teeth on a niblick. They owed much to J. H. Taylor. He was the first professional they saw and became their early model. Reginald's style was incisive, nothing fancy, just a quick address, abbreviated swing and the ball was despatched down the fairway. His grip was just as natural, an interlock with the left thumb outside.

Jointly their playing record was impressive. As club professionals, each could look back on long careers. Ernest at Meyrick Park, Charles at Crews Hill, and Reginald at Parkstone. They had a long association with the Ryder Cup. Charles, apart from playing in all six before the war, was an admirable British captain. A match-play specialist, the records show him as twice winner, runner-up and semi-finalist. Reginald hit the high spots in stroke competition. Ernest taught his brothers how to play. He lacked the rugged personality of Reginald, but nevertheless could look back on a good tournament career. He defeated George Gadd in the 1924 match-play final, but had to wait twelve years before reaching the same stage, when a youthful Dai Rees proved too much of a handful. I associate Ernest with the 1924 Open at Hoylake, a championship that developed into a cut-and-thrust affair between the West Country professional and the flamboyant Walter Hagen. When the last round began Ernest had a wonderful chance of returning a winning score. Maybe he tried too hard. Strokes were wasted on the early holes. He rallied over the fierce Hoylake finish, carding 78 and a total aggregate of 302. Hagen had similar trouble. The outward half cost 41 strokes. Level fours were then needed. Hagen succeeded by the narrow margin of one stroke.

Charles had a similar experience at Muirfield in 1935. His first two rounds of 71 and 68 were copybook stuff. A third of 73 was useful until Alfred Perry returned a sensational 67 for a one-shot lead. The last round was disastrous for Charles. Putts refused to drop. Seventy-six left him five shots behind Perry and one more than Padgham. His Ryder Cup tally was impressive. Charles was not on a defeated side in five foursome matches, winning twice and halving three times.

The Whitcombes occupied a warm corner in the esteem of their fellow professionals, particularly for their unswerving support of the artisan golf movement. They were rough diamonds, down-to-earth professionals, who would have little in common with the current breed. They typified the spirit of the Thirties.

Alfred Padgham's Year

The same might be said of Alfred Padgham. Here was a professional of the same school, remembered as a phlegmatic, poker-faced personality with an ideal temperament for the game. Nothing ruffled or upset him, and his outward serenity permeated his whole game. He was the ideal golfer to watch. The lazy power of his long game, the leisurely way in which the club was taken back in a controlled three-quarter swing, massive hands wrapped round the club as if the shaft was a matchstick, the surprisingly light grip – all could be studied and analysed in a way that was impossible with a fast swinger.

1936 was the year when everything went well for Padgham. Nothing could go wrong. By the time he arrived at Hoylake for the Open Championship, virtually every tournament had been won. Prior to that he was sadly below form. In the first tournament he only qualified by sinking a long putt on the last green. After that came the long run of success, due in main to his putting. The method used can easily be copied. He stood a long way from the ball, used an overlap grip with the back of the left hand facing the line of the putt and arms away from the body; the putt was played like a short chip, crisply and boldly. It worked miracles and made him Open champion. His long iron shots were also impressive, but to play them with such firm crispness and lazy deliberation calls for exceptional strength in forearms and wrists, muscular development that does not happen by chance.

Alfred Padgham was a traditional professional of the Thirties. His unruffled style impressed, yet looking back I recall not the many successes but an unorthodox shot that almost had dire consequences. We were playing in Vittel on a course that served as a steeplechase-cum-links. Padgham's tee-shot came to rest by a thicket-jump. An ordinary swing was impossible. Not having a left-handed club, Padgham straddled the ball with his back to the hole and played a full shot between his legs. Theoretically it should have finished on the green. Instead a fluffed shot almost had disastrous consequences in more senses than one.

Alfred Perry

On the grounds of unorthodoxy, Alfred Perry must be remembered. Here was a natural golfer in every way. This was demonstrated in the Open at Muirfield in 1935, a links that demands respect. Not so with Perry. His

Alfred Perry, 1935 Open Champion, had a highly individualistic style.

slashing, almost agricultural style was a joy to watch. There was nothing elegant about it. Using an unusual underhand grip with the right hand, standing a long way from the ball, he employed a full, uninhibited swing and lashed into the ball with pure abandon. To win the Open title calls for consistency, particularly at Muirfield, but seldom have these difficulties been so confidently brushed aside. As famous players faltered in that last round, Perry went from strength to strength, taking risks that came off, like the time he audaciously took a spoon out of a bunker to find the green. The margin of his win by four shots from men like Henry Cotton, Lawson Little, Henry Picard and Alfred Padgham proved that carefree flamboyancy can pay dividends provided the skill is there. Alfred Perry was such a golfer, the cavalier of pre-war style.

Carnoustie featured prominently. It is different, in a class of its own. Lacking the style of Prestwich or Troon, it is nevertheless an exacting test of golf: the overall impression is flatness, unless gentle undulations count. Water is the menace, a liquid network of potential danger titled Barry Burn and Jockie's Burn culminating at the 18th. Here the Barry Burn has to be crossed twice. The drive has to be placed on a peninsular roughly fifty yards wide, enclosed by a loop of the stream, with the green ahead again guarded by the burn measuring at least twenty-five feet across the front of the green. Under normal conditions it is tough enough, but in wind and rain the toll is heavy. This was highlighted in the two Open Championships held there in the Thirties.

Tommy Armour

In 1931 it was the turn of Tommy Armour, an Edinburgh Scot who went to America in 1922 and liked it so much he settled there, first as secretary at the Westchester-Biltmore Club, then he turned professional with considerable success. In 1927 he won the United States Open at Oakmont and had the reputation of being an exceptionally fine iron player. In the opening rounds at Carnoustie, his game was steady but not brilliant. Even so, it was good enough to keep pace with men like Henry Cotton, Johnny Farrell, Macdonald Smith and Gene Sarazen. More threatening was the sustained challenge by Jose Jurado. It was to become a repeat performance of the 1928 Open at Sandwich only to falter with a last round of 80. The South American was more consistent in 1931. Galleries were won over by his charismatic personality along with the Prince of Wales, a keen observer and supporter. After three rounds Jurado led on 220. Macdonald

Smith was 3 shots behind, whilst third place was shared by Tommy Armour, Gene Sarazen and Percy Allis on 225; Cotton dropped out of contention with a disappointing 79. Armour set a hot pace with a final 71 leaving Jurado needing 75 to win. Putts refused to drop. Everything turned on the last hole. The drive was copybook, but tactics cost the title. Instead of going for the pin, he played safe and left the iron short. The pitch was useful but by no means dead. He needed one too many to tie. Afterwards he said that had he known what was needed, a bolder second might have done it. It is difficult to believe that Jurado could have been so out of touch. Tommy Armour benefitted and was a worthy champion. He had a habit so mindful of Lee Trevino today. He was an incorrigible chatterer.

Henry Cotton's Finest Hour

In 1937 the Open returned to Carnoustie where Walter Hagen described the American entry as that country's most formidable onslaught on our title, hardly encouraging in the light of recent showings. In 1929 there were eight Americans in the first ten, whilst in 1933 they had five in the first six. This time Carnoustie had been stretched to over 7,000 yards and proved no respector of reputations. Sarazen and Hagen failed. Manero, the 1936 US Open champion, could not cope. Guldahl was out of sorts with his irons. Snead and Nelson gave glimpses of what was to come. Shute looked a threat. Opening rounds of 73 recalled how four 73s were good enough for victory at St Andrews five years earlier, but such hopes were drowned in the Barry Burn on the last day. Ed Dudley delighted with his lazy swing and equable temperament, but it could not survive the rigours of that last day. Atrocious conditions with gale-force winds and sheeting rain decimated the field. Flooded greens came near to play being abandoned. The man whose devastating golf ignored the storm was Henry Cotton. Of his many successes in a long career, I rate his final round as the finest of all. It contained only one mistake, a pushed iron shot at the home hole. Otherwise it was copybook. The details are worth recalling:

Out: 4-3-4-4-4-4-5-3-4—35
In: 4-4-4-3-4-5-3-4-5—36—71

Two strokes behind Cotton came Reginald Whitcombe, whose storm-taking efforts went a long way towards throwing the Americans out of their stride. This time not only was the champion a home player, but three

Henry Cotton represented the best that Britain has produced in international golf. His approach to the game was methodical and tireless. He set an example that was copied by every aspiring golfer. He reflected the will to win.

of the first four and six of the first nine places were occupied by our men.

This Open confirmed Cotton as being the most interesting golfer in the country. He had never been a natural golfer, yet somehow he hid the fact by concentrated effort and concentration. At the outset he advocated hitting from the inside out. At Carnoustie his shots were invariably straight with never a fade to the right, with just a hint of bending to the left. It was an impressive swing, its very fluency concealing the immense power infused into the shot. On the green the rhythm was unbroken. He was the complete golfer.

The Oldest Amateur Champion

The 1933 Amateur Championship at Hoylake was memorable for a different reason. The winner, the Hon. Michael Scott, became the oldest man to win the title, breaking the record set by Charles Hutchins, who became Amateur Champion at the age of fifty-three, the venue again being Hoylake. Born in 1878, Michael was a member of an eminent golfing family, with two brothers, Osmond and Denys, and their sister, Lady Margaret Scott, who as a girl inscribed their name three times on the Ladies Championship trophy. Her brothers tried in vain to match the honour. Osmond came nearest, losing 3 and 2 against A. G. Barry in the 1905 Amateur final at Prestwick. Time had run out. Michael, although in the veteran class, continued to enter for the championship almost as a token gesture. As a younger man his record was good, including the championship of Australia and France, as well as creditable showing in the Open Championship, but all that was a long time ago.

At Hoylake circumstances were not in his favour. The links had been stretched to over 7,000 yards, and entailed an extra 1,000 yards through having to walk back to the new tees. It was tough going for ageing legs. Scott quietly got into his stride, striking the ball with a low trajectory swing that gave plenty of run on the hard-baked fairways. His iron play was crisp, his mashie-niblick shots of sheer artistry, and his putting smooth and confident. One by one opponents were picked off, until the semi-final where he came up against an American regarded by many as the potential champion. George Dunlap's record was impeccable, having just won the American Amateur Championship and played in the US Walker Cup team. He was a delightful personality, effervescent and bubbly with enthusiasm. During a practice round I thought his style somewhat unorthodox, but the results were consistently impressive. He had shown what he could do against Lister Hartley, seven holes from the seventh in one over threes. His match against Sandy Somerville promised to be the highspot of the Championship. The Canadian had won the American Amateur title at Baltimore the year before; taking an early lead, he seemed to have the measure of his opponent, but it was Dunlap who struck two decisive blows – 4 at the 16th with a superb shot over the Cop from the rough to the green, followed by a 3 at the 17th.

The odds were stacked against Scott in the semi-final, conceding thirty-one years and unable to match his opponent's length from the tee. The handicap on such a championship links looked too much. Such fears were confirmed when Scott faltered on the greens and stood 2 down with 6 played. Consistency paid off. It began with a couple of 3s; with 4 holes to play he was 3 up, outplayed the American at the long 15th, and all was over.

Scott's opponent in the 36-holes final was Dale Bourn, again much younger. Pundits who reckoned that tiring legs over a second round might prove too big a handicap were silenced. With the air of an elderly golfer quietly enjoying a Sunday afternoon round, Scott methodically mastered his challenger and went into lunch with the luxury of a 5-hole lead. In the afternoon there was a momentary hiccup. Three putts at the first and rough at the 2nd cost two holes, but the systematic wearing-down attrition left Dale beaten at the 15th. The loser had the unusual experience of being runner-up in the English and British Amateur Championships in the same season.

For Michael Scott it had been a memorable week with a fitting reward for a famous family. Fifty-seven years later I received a charming letter from the son of Denys Scott. In it he wrote:

In June there will be great celebrations of our 125th Anniversary at the Royal North Devon Golf Club at Westward Ho. Among the Scott relations participating will be Harold and Eric Osmond Scott, one of the triumvirate of those great amateur golfers, Michael, Osmond and Denys. My brother Jack and cousin Harold are competing in the *Over 80's Championship* which brought a storm of protest from these two 'oldies', who felt deeply insulted at being asked to play a mere five holes! The Club have got round this by having an *Over 75s Competition* in which the *Over 80s* may play 18 holes, but only five holes may count for their Championship. I shall be able to compete in the *Over 75s* as I am 78 in April – a young 'rabbit' compared with my peers. Incidentally, we are hoping to arrange a *Scott Veterans'* contest against the Club in which four of us (average age 80) will play singles and foursomes over two days. We have done this over a number

RIGHT The Hon. Michael Scott had just become the oldest player to win the Amateur Championship. In the 1933 final at Hoylake this soberly dressed fifty-five-year-old veteran beat Dale Bourn by 4 and 3, quietly playing shots as if he was engaged in a Sunday-afternoon match.

BELOW Lawson Little, an American with awesome power who destroyed James Wallace in the Amateur final at Prestwick by 14 and 13.

of years and have usually managed to defeat them, though it is a far from serious occasion and accompanied by a lot of banter and consumption of much food and drink!

At least that brings us up to date with the happenings of the Scott family.

Returning to that final of 1933 I recall how George Dunlap watched every hole, giving warm support and encouragement to his conqueror. The following day he set off for St Andrews in a battered second-hand car he had bought on the Wednesday. Next to him sat his attractive wife, Kay, looking a trifle too smart for such a vehicle. After two breakdowns they eventually reached Rusacks. After the Open Championship the antique was given by George to his caddie.

Lawson Little

Another pivotal figure of the Thirties was Lawson Little, the American who won the British Amateur title in 1934 and 1935 and held the United States Amateur Championship in the same two years, turned professional and proceeded to win the American Open, a remarkable record of the most intimidating striker of the ball in this decade. He was as strong as an ox, broad shoulders, at the top of a shut-faced backswing, the latent aggressive power signalling that the ball would be belted out of sight. His opponent in the final, James Wallace, experienced the blast in no uncertain fashion. The Troon artisan, who had never been seriously considered by the selectors, confounded critics by knocking out five Walker Cup players on the way to that last day. Sadly the result was annihilation. Play began with an early start so that Little could catch the boat to America. The precaution was hardly necessary. On the first green Wallace required 3 putts. The American's lead was never relinquished. His figures on the morning round speak for themselves:

4-3-3-4-3-3-5-4-4 = 33 out
4-3-5-4-3-4-3-4-3 = 33 home

66 was 3 shots better than the record established at Prestwick by Macdonald Smith in the Open Championship of 1925. Twelve up at lunch, the pressure was kept up in the afternoon. At the first a 10-yard putt went down for a win in 3; the end mercifully coming at the short 5th. Ten under fours and 6 under par for the 23 holes. Poor Wallace struggled

gamely, but was swept away by the barrage. The boat was caught with time to spare!

Little's defence of the title the next year at Lytham was not so shattering. In the final his opponent was Dr William Tweddell, a resolute golfer, but on this occasion a semi-invalid on vacation having entered light-heartedly as part of a rest cure. It was an unusual convalescence. On paper it seemed a non-event. Tweddell, outdriven at times by eighty yards, had to use woods against the American irons. His unorthodox style was hardly reassuring but he held on with limpet-like tenacity. He lost 3 of the first 4 holes, 4 down at the 8th, the same margin at the 15th, but Tweddell clung on. It went to the 36th hole. The American deserved his win, but he had to fight hard.

Leonard Crawley

Another golfer I associate with the Thirties was Leonard Crawley, a member of a remarkable sporting family. Harrow and Cambridge preserve the records of his cousins' and uncles' feats. His talents as a true all-rounder were considerable without ever seeming to exhaust his resources. He gained a Blue for rackets as well as golf and cricket, won the Northern Lawn Tennis Doubles Championship partnering his uncle, earned a gold medal for ice skating, was a fine shot and had a rare understanding of gun dogs. He possessed a driving singleness of purpose that would not let him rest until he reached his goal. Cricket was perhaps his first choice. Had he persevered, Crawley would assuredly have played for England. He was asked if he could be available to tour Australia in 1932–3. Before that he went to the West Indies with the MCC in 1925–6 and there was speculation whether he would be chosen for G. O. Allen's team to Australia in 1936. In 1921 he made a century for Harrow against Eton at Lord's and played three times for Cambridge in the University Match. His best innings was 176 not out for Essex against Sussex at Leyton during which he twice hit Maurice Tate over the pavilion roof.

As a golfer Crawley won the English Championship in 1931 and was runner-up in 1934 and 1937. Among many victories were four wins in the President's Putter, Worplesdon Foursomes three times, the Berkshire Trophy, Royal and Ancient Spring and Autumn Medals, four appearances in the Walker Cup, more than seventy home internationals for England and runner-up in the 1937 French Open Championship against a strong professional entry. One victory was missing. Crawley would have made a magnificent Amateur Champion.

Crawley could be charming, eccentric and absent-minded. His personality did not readily project in forms of extroverted bonhomie, though at times his taste in clothes was unusual and he fancied himself in a ten-gallon stetson. He took some understanding, rather like getting to grips with the Albert Hall. He had a wry, pungent sense of humour that could be highly personal, and he was essentially an individualist, externally phlegmatic and as hard as perspex. Perhaps the finest tribute that can be paid to his memory is that the name and personality of Leonard Crawley will long be remembered in the annals of the game. He personified the image of an Edwardian sportsman, an anachronistic legend.

Crawley was also a participant in the historic Walker Cup match at St Andrews in 1938. The British record in this event was appalling. Another disaster would have raised the question of the advisability of persisting with such a one-sided contest, but, in spite of our lamentable record, the Americans were not taking chances. A young but immensely strong team, headed by Francis Ouimet, sailed on the SS *Bremen* of the North German Lloyd line, bound for the Amateur Championship at Troon as a curtain-raiser to the Walker Cup match. Today most of these American names are forgotten. Apart from Ouimet, already a golfing legend, Johnny Goodman was their outstanding player. This chunky little man from Omaha was the natural successor to Bobby Jones, who had retired after the Grand Slam. Goodman had already achieved the rare feat for an amateur of winning the American Open Championship. At Portland in 1937 I watched him complete the double by beating Ray Billows for the American Amateur title. A finely balanced match ended with Goodman winning on the last green. He promised to be a threat at St Andrews. He was conscious of his record and made sure that his opponents knew it.

Then there was Johnny Fisher of Cincinnati, long-legged, reticent, with crew-cut hair, a long slashing hitter with a very fast swing. He used to bend over as he addressed the ball, long arms coming through low and close to the body. He strode along on stilt-like legs at a fair pace and wasted no time fiddling about: in every way a magnificent golfer. Many of the others were equally impressive, including Bud Ward, who became American Amateur champion the next year, Charlie Yates, the happy-go-lucky protégé of Bobby Jones at Atlanta, and Charles Kocsis, with rhythmic swing and style. In retrospect these players were characters in their own right. It was a world apart. It is tempting to recall the 1938 Walker Cup match and compare it with those of recent years. It is impossible. Everything was so different. We have become blasé with Concorde shrinking space, television taking the world into the home, and taxation with inflation affecting every walk of life. In 1938 income tax was raised by the April Budget to 5s. 6d. The bank rate was two per cent. The pound was worth 4.80 dollars. Top-grade petrol was raised by 1d to 9d per gallon. Instead of James Bond we had Bulldog Drummond. The first-class fare to America on the *Queen Mary* was £64. The British navy was the largest in the world, outweighing the US Navy by nearly 300,000 tons, and the Russian Fleet was one-sixth the size of the British Navy.

In matters sporting, our Test cricketers made current counterparts look like selling-platers. Len Hutton scored 364 runs of the England total of 903 for 7 declared. Verity finished the season with 155 wickets for an average of 15.58. Donald Budge won the Wimbledon singles title for the second year, and Helen Wills Moody beat Helen Jacobs 6-5, 6-0 to take the ladies' title for the eighth time. Max Schmeling was thrashed in one round by Joe Louis in New York. If we wanted to escape from reality we could be entertained by Debroy Somers, Duke Ellington, Glenn Miller and Benny Goodman. In so many ways life was easier in those days but we did not realize it. One thing was certain ... we had a headache with the Walker Cup.

The First British Walker Cup Victory

To wipe out the memory of nine successive defeats, a clean sweep had been made of the old Selection Committee. The new men were Cyril Tolley, John Morrison, T. J. Thirsk, W. B. Torrance, and Dickson. They worked hard and eventually chose a cross-section of talent, with John Beck as captain. Again the names mean little to the present generation. There was bespectacled Cecil Ewing, a giant of a man who wielded a 17-oz driver as though it was a toy club. His irons were even heavier. Using a three-quarter swing and standing with feet close together, he slashed the ball immense distances, the force almost rivalling his rigid political principles. Hector Thomson, of a quiet, retiring disposition, had won the Amateur title two years earlier by beating the Australian Jim Ferrier by two holes at St Andrews. The rest were a rare mixture of temperaments and backgrounds. Harry Bentley displayed a Northern wit funnier than he realized. Gordon Peters and Alex Kyle reflected the dour humour of Glasgow. Leonard Crawley caricatured himself, which was by no means easy. Frank

Pennink was cool and reserved. Charles Stowe was a natural, uninhibited Midlander. James Bruen seemed oblivious of his skill and power.

On paper they looked a workmanlike side, nothing brilliant, but sound and dour, though lacking the charisma of their opponents. Then overnight the mood changed. All of a sudden there was a sparkling spirit of confidence. The trial matches did the trick. Not only did players from varying backgrounds get to know each other, but the transformation was largely due to the supervision of Henry Cotton, then at the peak of his career. Even his presence was reassuring. Here was no theoretical instructor, no pseudo-golfing doctor who could only talk and not perform, but one of the finest professionals this country has produced, who had a knack of instilling confidence in those he played with. In the trial matches he played with every member of the team in turn. Most important were his games with James Bruen.

The nineteen-year-old Irish youngster hit the headlines. Exceptionally strong, with powerful shoulders, he played off +6 against the Standard Scratch Score, with golf breathtaking in its force and accuracy. His style was unorthodox, with a loop at the top which somehow triggered itself in the downswing for the club came squarely to the back of the ball. The shots were high-carrying with a flight from the right. Wrist action was flawless. At impact the ball was given a tremendous blow. The results spoke for themselves. In those days it was unusual for 70 to be broken on the Old Course. Bruen played eight consecutive rounds, all ranging from 69 to 66, any four of which would have won any Open Championship played at St Andrews. The effect on the rest of the team was remarkable. It meant an immediate raising of standards. Seventy was made the norm. That was the mood when the day arrived.

Incidents stand out. Bruen was not in an all-conquering mood, but he had already played his part, and in Bentley had an excellent partner. They seemed to have the measure of Fisher and Kocsis, but in the end settled for a half. Peters and Thomson had the edge on Goodman and Ward. Kyle and Stowe could not get to grips with Yates and Billows, but Crawley and Pennink made no mistake against Smith and Haas. We ended the day with the precious lead of one point.

Beck, whose captaincy and judgment proved invaluable, made an unexpected move in the singles. Instead of dropping Kyle, he rested Bentley, in spite of his outstanding contribution in the foursomes. The gamble worked, though there were shocks and surprises galore. Pennink had his spirit broken and was thrashed to the tune of 12 and 11 by Ward, who had a morning round of 67, a halfway lead of 9 up, then resumed in the afternoon with 4-4-3-3 and all was over. Yates, who had won the Amateur title at Troon, continued in the same vein against Bruen, but Thomson had the better of Goodman. Peters and Kyle were shaping well, while Crawley established a useful lead over Fisher.

After lunch cracks began to appear. Crawley had Fisher slinging at him no fewer than six consecutive threes from the 26th to the 32nd. The American finished the match needing two fours for a 66. Stowe had a fierce struggle against Kocsis, survived, then had a purple patch and won by 2 and 1. Thomson, Peters and Kyle collected the points, Ewing and Billows came to the last green. The Americans tried for a three and failed, but by then it was academic. We had won the Walker Cup for the first time by three points. After years of failure, the Cup was ours. The strength of American golf had been trounced. Since then there have been further victories against the United States, but nothing can take away the memory of that moment at St. Andrews.

The Impregnable Quadrilateral

The Old Course is linked with one of the greatest golfers of all time. 1930 saw the unbelievable become fact and golfing history made when Bobby Jones won the Open Championship at Hoylake, the American Open Championship at Interlachen, the Amateur Championship at St Andrews and the American Amateur Championship at Merion, plus a clear 13-stroke victory at a professional tournament in Augusta, and his 36-hole Walker Cup match at Sandwich. Jones played competitive golf on both sides of the Atlantic from April to September and never finished below first place. To name him as the greatest golfer of all time might be queried by the skills of such men as Vardon, Hagen, Cotton, Hogan, Nicklaus and Ballesteros. Comparisons are impossible. Champions of different generations use different equipment and compete under different conditions. I think Jones' comments were applicable. 'I think we must agree that all a man can do is to beat people who are around at the same time that he is. He cannot win from those who came before, any more than he can win from those who come afterwards.' True words, but I believe the Atlanta amateur's record more than justifies the nomination.

To get his record in perspective it is useful to outline something of Jones's record. The basis of his classical swing and its rhythm came from Stewart Maiden, a Carnoustie-born professional who laid the foundation of his

Plaque set in bunker face on Lytham course to commemorate a significant bunker shot played by Bobby Jones in his Open Championship victory.

Bobby Jones (centre) congratulates Charles Coe for being low amateur in the Master's at Augusta. On the right is Ben Hogan who had won the Tournament with an aggregate of 280.

game and was at hand throughout his career. The style was unmistakable, an effortless flowing Scottish swing, almost lazy in its execution. It looked natural but was the result of almost microscopic analysis, in contrast with Maiden's methods which were simplicity itself, as Jones confirmed. 'It seemed that he merely stepped up to the ball and hit it, which to the end of my playing career was always a characteristic of my play.'

Statistics are silent, not only about a player's style, but his temperament. The American was a curious mixture. He was highly strung and the strain of competing exacted a toll on health and weight. Often during a championship he was unable to eat and became physically sick, yet no sign of this inner struggle was apparent. He personified unruffled calm. His precision shotmaking was a joy to watch. In contrast to the flamboyant flourishes of Walter Hagen, the lazy rhythm of Jones' swing was almost effortless, yet the amateur subjected his game to microscopic analysis, his theories to writing. In essence it makes good reading, maybe too metaphysical for some tastes for introspection can be taken too far. More interesting are his instructional films, visual presentations of historic value.

Pin-pointing a single round is difficult. The last eighteen holes at Hoylake in 1930 were tense after Archie Compston had carded a third round of 68, but on the home stretch the challengers failed until only Macdonald Smith was left with the challenge of having to hole-out in two to tie. The brave effort did not succeed. But my choice goes to the seventeenth at St Andrews in the Amateur Championship final against Cyril Tolley. Jones's second shot to the green was a talking-point for years. To appreciate its significance it must be remembered that spectator control then was more flexible than it is today. The gallery was not penned behind the famous road. Jones aimed deliberately to the left in the direction of the eighteenth tee. The ball struck a spectator and dropped safely out of trouble. I let Bernard Darwin's words take up the story: 'Hundreds are prepared to take the oath that it would otherwise have been on the road, and an equal number of witnesses are quite certain that it would not.' Tolley was not so fortunate. Obliged to go for the green, he found the dreaded Road bunker. The flag was between him and the road. He played a shot which Jones declared had 'never been surpassed for exquisitely beautiful execution.' Some years later Tolley told me that he thought Jones took a calculated decision, struck a low shot that was bound to hit a spectator with the obvious advantageous result. If that was so, the tactic was acceptable; then, with the help of a stymie, Jones won at the nineteenth and went on to make history.

Cyril Tolley won the first Amateur Championship after the First World War. Everything about his game was majestic. Such was his prowess that he was expected to win, in that sense he was a victim of his own sterling qualities.

Alfred Padgham was the most phlegmatic, poker-faced personality to win the Open. The keynote of his game was the absence of tenseness. Seen here with his father.

Conversation piece: Charles Littlefield, Francis Ouimet, Max McCready and John Beck.

The two outlines of Bobby Locke.

Bobby Jones was a man of many parts. As a scholar he had first-class honours in Law, English Literature and Mechanical Engineering. He had a legal practice in Atlanta, Georgia. With Clifford Roberts he planned and developed the Augusta National course and inaugurated the Masters' Tournament. In 1956 Jones was made an Honorary member of the Royal and Ancient Golf Club. Two years later he was non-playing captain of the American team in the inaugural match for the Eisenhower Trophy, and during that visit he was given the Freedom of the Burgh of St Andrews. He received it from a wheelchair to which he had been confined for many years because of a spinal complaint. He died on 18 December 1971. At the memorial service in St Andrews, the congregation included all representative golfing officials. One final tribute was the decision to name the tenth hole on the Old Course after this famous amateur golfer, who was so beloved and respected in St Andrews. He once said that if he had been obliged to live in one place and play golf there only for the rest of his life, he would have chosen the Old Course. He went on record: 'In my humble opinion, St Andrews is the most fascinating golf course I have ever played. There is always a way at St Andrews, although it is not always the obvious way, and in trying to find it, there is more to be learned on this British course than in playing a hundred ordinary American golf courses.'

The decade ends with a hard-luck story. I always felt sorry for Craig Wood, the American who won a fair share of tournaments but is remembered for the events he lost. Every one of the four major championships slipped from his grasp. In the American Open of 1939, Bryon Nelson outlasted him in the play-off. Gene Sarazen's historic double-eagle cost him the 1935 Masters. The PGA of 1934 he lost in the final to Paul Runyan. In the Open of 1933 Densmore Shute beat him in a 36-hole play-off. Near-misses discourage most fellows, but Craig took each disappointment with such grace that he became a favourite of the golfing public as America's No. 1 runner-up, a mantle later to be inherited by Ben Crenshaw.

IO

How Two Great Tournaments Began

THE President's Putter meeting was first held in 1920. The main idea of this meeting was to give the members of the Oxford and Cambridge Golfing Society an opportunity of getting together and talking over old times, and also, of course, playing some pleasant golf. Previously the members of the society had little chance of meeting each other except when playing in the various matches against golf clubs, and for various reasons, one of which was that they were not good enough players, many members were never invited for these matches.

The first winner was E. W. E. Holderness, who was also the second, the third and the fourth. In 1920 he beat Evan Campbell in the final by 6 and 4, Cyril Tolley in 1921 by 3 and 1, A. J. Boyd in 1922 by 6 and 5, and Cyril Tolley again in 1923 by 2 holes. In my opinion Ernest Holderness was one of the finest amateur golfers produced in the British Isles from 1919 onwards. Some of his closest friends doubted whether he would ever win the amateur championship, not because of his golfing ability but because of his nervous temperament. A. C. M. Croome held other views: 'Dammit, with a swing like that you can't play a bad shot, however nervous you may be.' Croome was right. Holderness first won the Amateur Championship in 1922 at Prestwick, when he beat John Caven on the 36th green. There was an enormous gallery all day, and when the final hole was played it was increased by hundreds lining the station wall, from which a good view could be obtained. This view, however, was not good enough for one spectator, who made certain of getting unrestricted sight of the play by climbing a signal post and clinging on to it like a monkey. Practically the whole of this enormous crowd had no desire to see Holderness win, not because they did not like him, but because he happened to be an Englishman, born in India, playing a Scotsman in Scotland. It is hard to imagine a situation more unfavourable to a man who suffers from nerves, yet Holderness, due to his sound methods, weathered the storm.

Playing with Holderness when he was at his best was certainly an education but also a disheartening performance. He was a superb driver; not only did every tee shot invariably go where he wanted it to, but it always went at approximately the same height. There have been many other good drivers, but the height of their shots has varied considerably. He won the Amateur Championship again at St Andrews in 1924, when he beat Eustace Storey in the final by 3 and 2. Shortly after this his work restricted the amount of time he could give to golf. He became president of the Surrey Golf Union and continued to win medals at Walton Heath. It should be noted that when he was winning his four consecutive victories in the putter, Tolley and Wethered were at their best. Tolley had won the Amateur Championship in 1920 at Muirfield, and Wethered tied in the Open Championship at St Andrews in 1921, and won the Amateur at Deal in 1923.

In 1924 his run of successes was broken by an original member of the society called Darwin, who became the first winner who had studied by the banks of the Cam. Of all the victories in the Putter this must surely be the most popular of all. Of his numerous successes on the golf course, this was one of Bernard Darwin's most satisfying achievements, and I have little doubt it gave him more pleasure than any of the others. Darwin was in his forty-ninth year, and cannot have been such a good player as he was when the wind continually caught his shots at the 19th at Hoylake and carried them out of bounds in an Amateur Championship, which he might have won. The weather at Rye that January was decidedly unfavourable to a man who was not as young as he used to be, but Darwin overcame all difficulties and beat O. C. Bristowe in the final by 4 and 2.

In 1925 a man who had helped to propel his college boat on the Cam won. The winner was Harold Gillies, known to the golfing world as Giles, and later to the young as Sir Harold. Gillies, like Darwin, was hardly in his prime as a golfer – he was in his forty-fourth year – but this did not stop him battling with the elements and his opponents. He defeated in the final no less a person than the first winner, Ernest Holderness.

Gillies was one of the originators of the Secretary's Niblick competition. This event is foursome play; partners are decided by lot and fight out by match play. Gillies assisted in the fashioning of the Secretary's Niblick itself. It always seems odd to me that the hands which had remodelled the faces of many grievously damaged by war or accident should have helped to fashion such a weird and ugly weapon as this unusual trophy. His efforts to get this competition started were rewarded in 1947, when he won it with Geoff Illingworth as his partner. The only others to have brought off the double of the President's Putter and the Secretary's Niblick have been Jim Peach and Laddie Lucas, who were considerably younger than Sir Harold.

It was not until 1926 that the post-Kaiser War golfers came into their own. Then Roger Wethered and Eustace Storey tied, play being abandoned due to darkness when the match stood at all square after 24 holes had been played. Various suggestions were made as to how the tie should be decided. One was that they should play off over a course in the vicinity of London. This clearly would not have been right or proper. The committee decided very wisely that they should hold the putter jointly for one year, a decision with which no sensible man would have disagreed. In the next two years Wethered won again, beating H. D. Gillies in 1927 by 2 and 1, and F. M. M. Carlisle in 1928 by 4 and 3. In 1929 Sir Ernest Holderness popped up again, and for the third time beat Cyril Tolley in the final, this time by 4 and 3.

I remember the final of 1930 because of a horse. In those days the Rye Golf Club possessed a horse, whose chief duty was to pull the mowing machine on the fairways. This was before Rye had taken to the modern gang mower, which, while essential for economical reasons, does not produce fairways as good as they used to be. In January no mowing of the fairways is necessary, and, having been a farmer, John Morrison felt it was only right that the horse should receive exercise. To repay the Rye Golf Club in some small way for the kindness it had always shown the Society, he considered it would be a nice gesture on his part to relieve them of the job of exercising their horse. He was delayed in the clubhouse after lunch on some business of importance with the cricket reporter of *The Times* and a distinguished member of the club, Captain Ravenhill. He was not able to pick the match up until the pulpit green which was then the 8th.

When Morrison arrived on his steed, which was far from fiery, Bourn's ball was on the green about 18 yards short of the hole, and Sir Ernest Holderness much closer. Bourn, who was the half-brother of J. S. F., took one look at his mount, roared with laughter, then gave his putt a sharp jab which sent it into the bottom of the hole. He thus won a hole he might easily have lost, and without doubt had a big bearing on the final result, 3 and 2 in favour of Bourn. Dale used to play like Hagen. He would hit several wild shots from the tee, followed by brilliant shots to the green with iron clubs of various lofts. After all, it did not matter very much where the tee-shots went if the seconds continually finished within seven yards of the the hole. Morrison said he was a little disappointed that he did not receive any official thanks from the secretary for exercising his horse. He had another disappointment when next he met Harry Colt, his partner in golf architecture. He gave him what was known in the services as a severe reprimand. With all his experience as a golf architect, Colt should have realized that horses had to have exercise, especially at that time when all new putting greens were formed by scoops pulled by horses.

The meeting of 1931 was played on ground frozen as hard as a board, and fog also interfered with play on the Saturday afternoon. Algy Pearson won, beating the great French golfer Andre Vagliano in the final by 6 and 5. Pearson dealt with the conditions better than his opponent and deserved his win, but to say his victory was not a surprise would be stretching a point. In 1932 Leonard Crawley gained the first of his three victories in this tournament, beating A. J. Evans in the final at the 21st hole. Johnny Evans managed to escape twice from the enemy in the First World War, but could not get away from Crawley in 1932 or Wethered in 1935. He set a splendid example to all golfers when he asserted his right in the Amateur Championship of 1929 at Royal St George's to go through the match in front, which had lost more than one clear hole on the previous pair. It was unfortunate that the match he went through happened to include the reigning Amateur Champion. Jim Peach is the only winner of the putter who never represented his university in the university golf match. Nevertheless, he thoroughly deserved his victory over Wethered in 1933.

In 1934 Ham Martin beat Rex Hartley in the final by 5 and 4, giving a wonderful exhibition how the game should be played in a real gale. The high tee close to the clubhouse was then in play and the wind was so strong that players could hardly stand on it. Martin, who had the build for a scrum-half, had the honour. He planted his feet firmly on the ground, hit a shot so well it took no notice of the gale. Poor Rex was blown off his feet at the top of his swing and missed his drive. The end was inevitable. In 1935 Wethered beat Evans 2 and 1, and did so again the following year by defeating Major Jumbo Aitken 2 and 1. The 1937 final went to the 19th before John Beck got the better of Ham Martin. In 1938 Cyril

Tolley at last broke through, beating Kenneth Scott by two holes after previously losing three finals. The year 1939 produced the youngest winner and probably the coldest meeting. Some people even slept in their dressing gowns. John Greenly, who had played for Oxford in 1935 and 1936, beat Ham Martin in the final by 4 and 3. It was a great performance for the youngster to beat such an experienced campaigner as Martin, especially as the latter knew every blade of grass at Rye and was usually at his best on these links. Outbreak of war interrupted the sequence, perhaps a timely moment to end early reminiscences of this prestigious event.

About 1923 a small party, including G. L. Mellin, known to all his golfing and football friends as Susie, and Halford Hewitt, was sitting in the palatial clubhouse of the Stoke Poges Golf Club endeavouring to put back into their bodies a little of what a strenuous day's golf had taken out. They were not discussing the SSS – in fact, at that time it had never been heard of – or the new code of rules, which in those days did not appear biannually, or anything to do with the game of golf. Their conversation was about association football, and especially about matches in the Arthur Dunn competition. Susie Mellin suggested that a golf competition run on the lines of the Arthur Dunn would be rather fun. The others considered this idea admirable, and Halford Hewitt said that if the competition could be arranged he would present a cup.

The originators had been footballers of distinction, and were fully convinced that games in which you play for your side were very much better for both the young and the old than golf, where in the majority of cases you play solely for yourself. The Halford Hewitt competition was to be a team affair and, to ensure this, it was decided that play should be by foursomes, that the teams should consist of five pairs, and that all matches should be played to a finish to avoid any possibility of a tie. The competition was first played in 1924 with an entry of only eleven schools, which included Eton, Harrow, Charterhouse, Winchester, Malvern, etc., and decided by play over 36 holes. The team out of the hat first could select the course on which their match should be played. Consequently several courses were used for the competition. In the final Eton beat Winchester at Addington by four matches to one.

From the small entry of 1924 it looked as if the competition might be a flop, but the next year, when it was played at Deal, the entry increased and continued to do so. There have been innumerable alterations and experiments to cope with the enormous entry but, throughout, the glorious spirit of a jamboree has been retained. It was a hectic weekend, the most stimulating golf meeting of the year, completed by Hal's luncheon to the winners, runners-up, and those fortunate to be invited, fleeting hours when Kummel and oratory flowed fast. There were incidents galore, enough to pack a volume. One refers to the little bridge that had the warning notice, 'Mind the Bridge'. Some didn't and suffered damaged heads, particularly for the captain of a distinguished team. He belted along in a car with half his side aboard and cleared the bridge at some 60 mph – half of his troops were concussed. The year when summer-time was advanced by a week, the 7 a.m. start being listed on the starting-sheet as 8 a.m., one competitor had the unusual experience of being eliminated from the tournament for good by breakfast-time; the experience of two people in the same hotel putting the clocks on independently of each other, resulted in early risers being hurried out of their beds one hour too soon. 1938 is recalled when an abnormally high tide crashed through the pebble ridge and flooded the course with shingle, flotsam and jetsam. Only a secretary with the equanimity of Bernard Drew and his excellent ground staff could have coped. Few sights are more invigorating than the club-house at the height of the Halford Hewitt, crowded with golfing personalities and the old boys of the public schools discussing golf, exchanging yarns, and living beyond their handicaps.

11

The Wind of Change

'THE WIND of change' was first detected by Harold Macmillan. His analysis was accurate. A similar assertion can be made about the post-Second War world of golf. We have had more than our share of a similar wind, penetrating mistrals, sluggish eddies, cooling breezes and sudden blasts. We live so close to the present that the cause and effect of these changes tend to be forgotten. Memories are short. Golfing happenings have altered the background, in certain respects completely changing it, and not always for the better. Up to now it is interesting to recall the names and feats of those who made the headlines over past decades. One way to assess achievements is to concentrate on the prestigious events in the golfing calendar, such as the Open Championship of Britain and America, the United States Masters, and the Amateur Championships of both countries. The roll-call of winners is a true indicator of the giants of each decade. The fingerprints of success are plain. From its inauguration in 1860 the Open has known spells of domination. The Morrises, father and son, and the Parks shared the honours until the years of the famous triumvirate of J. H. Taylor, James Braid and Harry Vardon. After the First World War came the golden years of Walter Hagen and Bobby Jones, then the multiple wins by Henry Cotton, Bobby Locke and Peter Thomson, succeeded by another invincible triumvirate of Arnold Palmer, Gary Player and Jack Nicklaus, and into the seventies with four great names, Jack Nicklaus, Gary Player, Lee Trevino and Tom Watson. An indication of the domination by this quartet in that decade is reflected by statistics. Between them, they won twenty-two of the forty-four major events. The balance was shared by fifteen golfers. Only four are non-American, Tony Jacklin (Britain),

Severiano Ballesteros (Spain), David Graham (Australia), and Gary Player (South Africa).

1970 was Tony Jacklin's year. His clear-cut victory by seven shots in the US Open at Chaska was a significant victory by an English professional on American soil. Likewise memorable was the victory by Sam Snead in the 1946 Open at St Andrews. It was appropriate that the first post-war Open was staged on the Old Course. Seven years earlier Richard Burton had won the title there, but because of hostilities was denied the expected rewards for such success. That period of competitive inaction on the fairways was reflected in the results. The first three places and six out of the first ten were occupied by overseas challengers. Even then pending changes were apparent. For the first time spectators were excluded from the playing area of the Old Course by barriers with crossing-points specifically marked. Many resented being regimented under the naive assumption that spectators had rights. Professionals were informed that prize money would be doubled. Alongside today's financial rewards, the amounts were barely pin-money. In 1946 the Open was valued primarily in prestige terms.

Sam Snead

The new Champion was a slim, youthful-looking Sam Snead, still behatted, with rounds of 71, 70, 74, 75, giving victory by four strokes, the largest margin since Alfred Perry won at Muirfield in 1935. Had chances not been frittered away in the final round, it could have been a different story. Six players were in contention. Dai Rees ruined everything in the first three holes. He began with his drive heading for the rails, striking a spectator and rebounding into play. The little Welshman then found the burn with his next shot. Seven went on the card. Three putts at the second; three putts at the third; 17 for three holes; 42 to the turn, total 80, and an aggregate of 295 left him level with Henry Cotton and Charles Ward, one ahead of Bobby Locke and Johnny Bulla. Snead came to the 18th tee needing 7 for victory. Only four shots were used. There were other memory vignettes: Sam King three-putting on seven greens and failing to qualify; Cyril Tolley tearing up his card on the New Course; Bobby Locke needing only one putt on seven greens in his opening round of 69; Dai Rees' record-breaking 67 in the second round: Charles Ward holing-out in one at the short 8th; but when the dust settled it was very much a Virginian triumph.

The graceful power of Snead's had a naturalness about the action

Sam Snead won every major championship except, ironically, the US Open.

that was near-flawless. He has won every major championship, except ironically the United States Open, being runner-up five times and third once. The roll includes the Open, three PGA titles, the Canadian Open Championship, Western, and three Masters Tournaments. Altogether he won some 112 Open Championships and tournaments. No one in tournament golf today can match Sam Snead's powerful presence on the fairways, yet he has always been unimpressed by his reputation as a major figure in golfing history.

Before the 1946 Amateur Championship many forecast that Frank Stranahan would be the winner. Others picked the like of Leonard Crawley, Alex Kyle, Cyril Tolley and John Langley. Ten days before the event I predicted in a broadcast that the fairways and sandhills of Birkdale could be a successful battleground for James Bruen. After many anxious moments the title eventually went to Saostat Eirean. Bruen became Champion with golf far below the standard we would have expected before the war. Youthful enthusiasm had gone. In America the Open Champion was Lloyd Magrum, Stanley Bishop held the Amateur title, Ben Hogan became PGA Champion, Herman Keiser won the Masters, and in Australia Ossie Pickworth reigned supreme.

Fred Daly

At Hoylake Fred Daly became the first Irish-born holder of the Open title after a dramatic finish. At the home hole of just over 400 yards, Frank Stranahan needed a 2 to tie. The American ruled the pin on a green large enough to 3-putt comfortably. Unhurried and unflurried, he watched the ball finish a few inches from the hole and Fred's name was engraved on the trophy. Had it not been for a slight hiccup in the third round when he carded 78, the margin would have been greater. This breezy Ulster golfer, who died in 1990, was one of the most popular on the circuit. Nothing ruffled him, at least outwardly. He whistled his way round the course and made golf seem a happy affair, which is more than can be said about some current professionals.

Willie Turnesa and Richard Chapman

The Amateur Championship at Carnoustie produced another record. For the first time the final was contested by two Americans, Willie Turnesa and Richard Chapman. Only the luck of the draw spared us the indignity of

Fred Daly winning his second Match-play Championship in successive years at Birkdale 1948. This breezy Ulster golfer, who won the Open at Hoylake, is remembered for his carefree approach to the game. Nothing ruffled him.

Frank Stranahan was cast in the same mould as Henry Cotton and Ben Hogan. His concentration was total. Seen here with Charles Stowe after winning the Amateur Championship.

seeing four Americans disputing the semi-finals. In 1948 Frank Stranahan beat Charles Stowe by 5 and 4 in the Amateur Championship at Royal St George's. It was a study in contrasts. Stowe had no pretensions to style. He just hit the ball in the most economical manner and to hell with appearances. No time was wasted, he just got on with the job of efficient shot-making. Stranahan's methodical, almost remorseless precision golf proved too strong. At Muirfield, Henry Cotton, aged forty-one, became Open Champion for the third time. My recollections are of narrow fairways, plenty of rough, and a scorching hot day when, in the presence of the reigning monarch and before a record-breaking crowd, Cotton returned an immaculate 66. That day we were privileged to see stroke production at its best. In America Ben Hogan likewise confirmed his superiority over his colleagues by winning the US Open.

1949 saw another Irish success when Max McCready broke the American monopoly in the Amateur Championship by beating Willie Turnesa 2 and 1 at Portmarnock. Like Daly and Bradshaw, McCready enjoyed golf. His victory was almost a one-off chore. Afterwards he was picked for Walker Cup and Irish team duties, but never again did he figure prominently in championships, maybe a light-hearted Irish streak refused to be curbed. Bobby Locke had the measure of Bradshaw in the Open at Sandwich, the result influenced by the dramatic 'bottle' shot described in Chapter 12.

So ended a decade that began with the phoney war, the Sitzkreig, with armies sitting in the Maginot Line and the Siegfried Line hardly firing a shot, almost repeated fifty years later in the slow build-up of forces in the Gulf. The German invasion, the Battle of Britain, Pearl Harbor; austerity prevailed. More mundane happenings ... postage increased from 1d to $2\frac{1}{2}$d, petrol went up to $1/11\frac{1}{2}$d. After 2,000 nights of black-out, we were ablaze with light, the price of victory and defeat being 55 million dead. Eros returned to Piccadilly Circus, and a packet of cigarettes went up to 3/4d. Everything spelt change.

12

The Hambledon of English Golf

IT IS interesting to piece together something of the background of club golfers of the past. For this purpose the Hambledon of English golf is Blackheath. Unfortunately there was no John Nyren to record the golfing happenings of three centuries ago. Like the fate of the old Lord's pavilion, invaluable minute books were destroyed by fire. Nevertheless from such existing fragmentary evidence, it is possible to reconstruct a scene which shows that club golfers, irrespective of the century, have much in common. Blackheath golfers met for play every Saturday, dining afterwards at the Green Man hotel. Their hospitality is evident by a description written by a former secretary:

The company assembled at two o'clock, and after walking in front of the tents for some time, the ladies were invited to partake of a cold collation, consisting of fowls, ham, fruits of various kinds, ices, jellies, cakes. Sir John Eamer's regimental band playing, and a party of his regiment keeping the ground in front of the tents, where the golf flag was erected. Two stewards attended each tent to wait on the ladies, who, after partaking of the refreshments, retired to accommodate the gentlemen, and walked the ground in front of the tents. The gentlemen soon joined the ladies, and the scene then became truly interesting from so large an assemblage of beauty and fashion.

It is difficult to imagine such 'goings on' today. Another entry in the club books describes a weekly dinner:

Saturday, October 18th, 1834 – The Club having observed that the 93rd Highlanders, on their march from Canterbury to Weedon Barracks, would pass our golfing ground, directed the Secretary to invite Col. McGregor and the officers

Frank Pennink. a stylish golfer who left his mark on the amateur scene.

Roberto de Vicenzo, the Argentinian professional who has the distinction of being the oldest player at 44 years and 93 days to win the Open. He doubtless remembers more vividly that day in Augusta when he lost the right to play off for the Masters title through signing his card for a four-hole which he did in three.

Colourful, controversial, colloquial ... the best way to describe these forthright professionals. Archie Compston, massive in frame, outspoken and direct in speech, was always noticeable. Norman von Nida was a tough little Australian with an outsize personality.

Johnny Goodman, a stocky little man from Omaha who became the natural successor to Bobby Jones. As an amateur he won the US Open, and completed the double when he beat Ray Billows for the US Amateur title.

of this distinguished regiment to dine with the Club, which invitation Col. McGregor accepted for as many officers as accompanied the staff of the regiment on this day. The Club had only to regret that so few appeared at the festive board. The Secretary announced that Charles Sutherland, one of our members, had taken unto himself a wife this morning, and that a very abundant supply of champagne and claret was presented to the Club by Mr and Mrs Sutherland on the occasion ... the company separated just in time to say they did not break the Sabbath.

Numerous entries appear in the records of 'gallons of claret'. Apart from bets for golf matches, a gallon of claret had to be paid whenever a member married or there was an addition to the family. Play must have been of a light-hearted nature for scores of 130 were common. The round at first was one of five holes, the lead of the Leith Club being probably copied. Later it was extended to seven holes, the test being three times round. It must have been fairly difficult for in the gutty days a score under 100 was considered respectable. The round began quietly with a short hole, followed by two of more testing nature, but not as long as the fourth and fifth, which measured respectively 550 and 520 yards. Many of the hazards were rich with tradition: Glennie's Hole, Sleepy Hollow, Marr's Ravine, not forgetting the water ponds, cart tracks and the windmill, later having to give way to lampposts, signboards, iron railings and seats, perambulators, nurserymaids and policemen, whilst the clubhouse, originally on the heath, became engulfed by bricks and mortar. Such was the congestion that a golfer had to wear a red coat and employ a fore-caddie.

Blackheath is the mother of English golf. Tradition dates its inception to 1608, being founded by James I of England and VI of Scotland, and his Scottish Court. Play then was probably confined to the portion of the heath by the Royal Manor of East Greenwich. Unfortunately documentary evidence is missing prior to 1800. The records really begin with the Silver Club given to the club by Dr Henry Foot in 1766, when golf was played on the heath in summer only, and over a course of five holes. The first written records of the game at Blackheath are dated 1787. A list of club members entered in the cash book of the Chocolate House at Blackheath shows names suggestive of Scottish descent. After that comes the bet book recording the fate of many a gallon of claret. The game continued to be played only in the summer months until 1789 when the Knuckle Club came into existence. In keeping with its odd name, members used to meet 'to discuss a dish of soup and knuckles, particularly the beef ones,' and an after-dinner speaker had to clutch a knuckle in his hand whilst speaking.

They adopted the brave policy of playing golf on the heath in winter. In 1825 the Knuckle Club became the Blackheath Winter Golf Club, and continued for nineteen years until 1844, when it merged with the older Summer Club. With the disappearance of the distinguished names came the Royal Blackheath Golf Club. To mark its decease, the Winter Golf Club bequeathed its challenge medal to the older club. Blackheath golfers played the game under their own rules. Unfortunately no written code of laws exists earlier than 1843. A change came in April 1892, when it was unanimously agreed that the Rules of Golf, as approved by the Royal and Ancient Golf Club of St Andrews on 29 September 1891, be adopted by the Royal Blackheath Golf Club, with the addition of certain local rules peculiar to the Blackheath Links.

13

The Saga of Sandwich

A CHAMPIONSHIP links that figures prominently in the history of the game is Royal St George's, Sandwich, a golfer's dream lay-out. It has everything: majestic dunes, terrifying carries, towering bunkers, even the consequences if shots fail. It is a test for giants. That fact created adverse criticism in the early days, particularly from golfers north of the Border. Sandwich was denigrated as a course for hitters that ignored the finesse of iron play. By comparison it fell short of St Andrews and Hoylake. In time it became accepted that Sandwich was intended by nature to be on the grand scale. Irregular surfaces meant improvised stances, blind spots, punchbowl greens and shots that kept their secret until the top of a hill was reached, all had to be accepted as part of the scene. Purists who expect every lie to be on a flat surface may grumble but it makes for entertaining golf. Today Royal St George's is a fitting test for world-class professionals, especially if the winds are fresh. When this ultimate hazard is present, the new champion will have earned his title the hard way, but the real Sandwich does not return until the crowds, the grandstands and all the commercial paraphernalia that are part of the current competitive scene have disappeared. Then and only then is the atmosphere restored. Solitariness is one of the charms of Sandwich with its tall and secret hills that unexpectedly yield the view of Pegwell Bay with the white cliffs and sparkling sea beyond. That is the picture that members cherish and has little in common with the fever of championship golf.

Royal St George's had the distinction of being the first English club to stage the Open Championship. That was in 1894 and it marked J. H. Taylor's first Open win. It was also Douglas Rolland's only appearance in this event. Starting as favourite, he lost to Taylor by five strokes. This marked the beginning of the Triumvirate domination. Between 1892 and 1914 there were twenty-three Open Championships out of which sixteen were won by J. H. Taylor, Harry Vardon or James Braid. That left only seven for the challengers. Harold Hilton won twice and the remaining five went to William Auchterlonie, Sandy Herd, Arnold Massey, Ted Ray and Jack White.

Taylor made no mistake at Sandwich, winning with an aggregate of 326 for 72 holes. Harry Vardon had to be content with fifth place. Cartoonists caught something of Taylor's pugnacious aggressiveness – chin jutting out and cap pulled well down – as he belted the ball into a gale-force wind. He was a specialist of the low flying shot and relied on the use of backspin which was then something of a novelty. It used to be said that such was his accuracy that the direction posts were almost a hazard. J. H. was an advocate of the open stance with the left foot at times well behind the right and almost pointing at the hole. It was an individualistic mannerism that suited his game.

In the 1899 Open at Sandwich, Harry Vardon was at his peak. He was tipped to win, a forecast that even his opponents accepted. Superiority with wooden shots proved a decisive factor. His style ran counter to orthodox theories: the club was lifted abruptly and straight, Vardon maintaining that an upright swing suited the gutty ball, particularly brassy shots. A speciality was a high-floating, quick-stopping shot. Vardon could reach most targets with two full woods against his opponent's two woods and a chip. Shots with a very heavy driving mashie were often on a par with a brassy, and the push-shot with a cleek was ideal for Sandwich. There was no trace of the traditional sweeping St Andrews swing. The clubs he used were considerably shorter and lighter. The famous Vardon overlapping grip was in reality shared with Taylor, who in turn had copied it from J. E. Laidlay.

Taylor used to say that Vardon was the only man he feared: not without cause, for it was Vardon who dethroned him. This was emphasized in the 1911 Open at Sandwich. George Duncan set an early pace. At the halfway stage he had a one-stroke advantage over Vardon, Ray and Taylor. Hilton was the leading amateur with 150. Edward Blackwell set a new course record with 71, later equalled by Duncan. In the third round Vardon posted an early 75 which left him three shots better than Taylor or Herd.

The last round saw Vardon falter. Out in 38 and home in 42 meant an aggregate of 303 which was distinctly vulnerable. Taylor and Herd could have forced a tie with 77. The weather played a significant role. As the wind increased, hopes were blown away. Hilton looked the best bet. Out in 33, he began the home stretch confidently but came unstuck with a 6 at the twelfth and 5 at the short sixteenth. Herd was the next. On the eighteenth he needed 4 to win but had to settle for a 6. Arnaud Massey required 4 to tie and duly obliged. The play-off was evenly contested at the outset, both players going out in 36. The breakthrough came at the fifteenth where Vardon carded 4 against Massey's 6 and went into lunch with the luxury of a five-shot lead over the Frenchman, increased to seven at the fifteenth in the afternoon. Massey conceded defeat on the seventh green. Vardon's six Open victories amounted to domination by a supreme genius. Up to the green he was in a class of his own. With a putter he became a competent performer rather than brilliant. Yet such was Vardon's mastery with woods and irons that putting often became a formality.

Jack White was typical of the early professionals. Born in 1873 at Pefferside in East Lothian, his childhood was spent playing around the links. As a boy of ten he caddied for J. E. Laidlay at North Berwick, inevitably using the amateur as his model, a style that influenced his game. Turning professional was an obvious step, his posts including York, Newmarket and Sunningdale where he stayed for twenty-five years. The odds against winning a major prize were enormous. Competing against the Triumvirate was like playing the best ball of Nicklaus, Norman or Faldo. It used to be said that White was too short from the tee to be taken seriously. This may have been true, but in the 1899 Open at Sandwich he overcame the strong wind to finish second to Vardon, helped by a brilliant short game and meticulous putting.

White's chance came at Sandwich in 1904. The entry of 144, including the Triumvirate, was the largest field the Open had attracted. Two days were set aside for the first eighteen holes. Robert Thomas led with 75, Jack Graham and Harry Vardon were one stroke behind with Tom Vardon, James Braid and J. H. Taylor bracketed together on 77. Harry Vardon carded 73 on the second round and led the field by three strokes. Jack Graham was second with 76, James Sherlock added 71 to an indifferent opening round of 83 to tie for third place with Tom Vardon. Harry Vardon slipped back with 79. James Braid took over with 69. Jack White was making steady progress. His halfway aggregate of 155 was followed by 72 which put him second on 227 with Harry Vardon one shot behind. Tom Vardon and J. H. Taylor were on 229.

In the final round, White set the pace, 69 and an aggregate of 296 became the target. J. H. Taylor and James Braid took up the challenge. Taylor returned 68 and Braid 69, but they had to be content with equal second. Braid had the satisfaction of having the lowest 36 holes of 71 and 69 in the Open. Victory went to Jack White, who became the first Open Champion to break 390.

Walter Hagen was always the master showman and he loved every minute of it. Stories about him are legion, many apocryphal, most of them true, some of which I have recorded elsewhere in this book. Nothing was impossible to such a likeable, impudent character. Arthur Croome wrote on his first arrival: 'It was at once borne in on me that here was a man who would not fail through excess of modesty.' His charisma was infectious. He lifted American professional golf out of a rut into financial plenty. His manager, Bob Harlow, once wrote: 'With a broad expansive grin on his features, Hagen looked at the world through a hole in the doughnut and kept his hands on the dough.' Hagen in turn wrote of Harlow: 'Through all those years we never had a written contract of any sort. He set up the dates, I played the tournaments and exhibitions and we carried the greenbacks away in an old suitcase. It was an ideal arrangement; it allowed me to relax and enjoy my friends and my game.' All very trusting, maybe not to the liking of Mark MacCormack of later years.

Hagen had an individualistic style, demonstrated in unforgettable fashion in his Open victories at Sandwich in 1922 and 1928. In the latter, two incidents affected the result. At the fifteenth in the last round Hagen found the cross-bunker with his second. A superb recovery and a single putt saved the day, a useful finish of 3–4–4 giving an aggregate of 292. Gene Sarazen, on the other hand, ruined his chances with a rash stroke. At the Suez Canal hole his ball found the rough from the drive. The caddie suggested an iron but Sarazen took wood, made a mess of the shot, then, without pausing, played the ball again with the same club. The result was poor. Latin blood had overruled commonsense.

It is unlikely that there will be another Walter Hagen. So dissimilar to today's professionals, he enjoyed his golf, and it showed.

Sandwich 1934 produced the first British win in the Open for ten years. It is true that the American invasion was not as strong as in previous years but the opposition was none the less formidable. Henry Cotton made the running. Like Hagen he possessed a magnetic personality, not outgoing like the American, but complex, concentrated, almost unapproachable. His perseverance was tireless, hours of back-breaking practice in search of near-perfection. The quality of the challenge was demonstrated in the qualifier when he returned 66. In the first round of the championship proper Cotton tamed the 6,700-yard links with a 67 and followed it with 65. His scorecard spoke for itself:

Out: 4–3–3–4–4–4–3–4–4
Home: 4–3–4–4–4–4–3–3–3

One hundred and thirty-two for 36 holes gave him a nine-stroke lead over Alfred Padgham, who had 72 and 70.

Conditions changed in the third round, scoring being made difficult by wind, rain and hail. 72 was respectable and only Joe Kirkwood with 71 was able to nibble the lead away by one shot. The final round was traumatic for Cotton. Something in the lunch disagreed with him. Violent stomach cramp made fluent golf impossible. He looked ill and felt frightful. In the circumstances 40 to the turn was a fine effort and 39 coming home gave an aggregate of 283 that equalled Sarazen's victory at Prince's in 1932. Sid Brews, the closest challenger, finished with five strokes too many. Henry Cotton had won his first Open Championship.

The first two days of the 1938 Open were played in perfect weather. Scores were low with Busson, Cox and Burton leading the way. When the storm broke, scores rocketed. The huge trade marquee was torn to shreds and the contents of the stands scattered everywhere. Cotton managed a 74. Reginald Whitcombe had a 75, two strokes better than James Adams, who recovered three shots on the ninth when Whitcombe needed four putts. Downwind, life was easy. Padgham drove the 380-yard eleventh and sank the putt for a 2. In the afternoon only rugged men like Whitcombe, Adams and Padgham were able to cope with the storm. The issue was virtually settled at the seventeenth where Whitcombe struck two raking shots into the wind followed by an accurate run-up and a single putt. Adams finished two shots behind to make him yet again the runner-up. Both men had played superbly in terrible conditions, Whitcombe with the short swing, Adams favouring the full sweep reminiscent of the old St Andrews swing. There was an outside chance that Cotton might manage a 71 to tie. Thirty-six going out and 4–3–3 on the homeward half showed it was possible but shots were dropped and 74 gave him third place. In calm weather Royal St George's is a stiff examination. In gale conditions only a truly great golfer can hope to succeed. Reginald Whitcombe was a great golfer.

Eleven years later the Open returned to Sandwich. Again the issue was wide open. Only after three rounds did the pattern take shape. Harry Bradshaw, Max Faulkner and Bobby Locke were level. Bradshaw had an immaculate fourth round of 70, which left only Locke likely to better. Out in 32, he was one stroke over the Irishman, but the advantage was lost at the tenth. Fives at the fourteenth and fifteenth, plus three putts at the sixteenth, blunted the assault but 3 at the seventeenth and 4 at the home hole enabled Locke to tie. The play-off was never a contest, Locke returning 67 and 68 to win by twelve strokes to give the South African his first Open success, one that might never have been but for a beer bottle. The incident happened at the fifth in the second round. Bradshaw drove into the rough, where the ball found its way into a beer bottle. The ruling on the 'unplayable ball' was specific: 'The ball is "unplayable" if the player considers he cannot make a stroke at it and dislodge it into a playable position.' Rather than chance disqualification, Bradshaw took an iron and played the ball where it lay. The bottle was smashed. The ball travelled about 40 yards. The par 4 hole cost 6, two vital strokes that would have made all the difference.

It was a pity because Bradshaw would have made the ideal non-conformist Open Champion. His grip was typical. The first two fingers of his right hand hung down like passangers and had little to do with the stroke. His alternative grip was the cross-handed effort, a relic of shinty days. He was the model example of not keeping the head still and his swing was somewhat agricultural. An average golfer copying it might become a hockey convert, yet the fact remained that Bradshaw made it work superbly. His was one of the most delightful personalities in the game and in semi-retirement ambled round the fairways in benign fashion. Like Hagen his kind has not been repeated.

The 1981 Open at Sandwich does not rank among the greatest in its long history but it produced in Bill Rogers a worthy champion whose manner and shot-making, particularly when the pressure was greatest during the last round, epitomized all that is good in the game. His popularity with the crowds was heart-warming. Sandwich came through the test with flying colours. At the outset there was a surprise. A few hours after arriving, Tom Watson complained that excessive watering of the course had changed its character. Royal St George's had been American-ized, green and lush. John Salvesen, the Royal and Ancient Championship Committee chairman, refuted the charge, pointing out that a rainfall of 2.4 inches in four days had left the links playing much slower. He was confident that the greens would have speeded up by the time the championship was under way. The prediction was right. The links provided a magnificent test, the severity of the examination being reflected in the high scores. During that week an interesting little ceremony recalled memories of that great golfer, Harry Weetman. His widow, Freda, arranged that a gold watch presented to her husband by Shropshire golfers be given to Sandy Lyle as the best Shropshire-born golfer at that time, coupled with the gift was the wish that in thirty years time he would pass it on to the player whom he considered the best Shropshire player in the year 2011. Lyle accepted the gift and its wish.

14

The Fifties Background

To RECALL the golf world of the Fifties is a nostalgic exercise. It is strange that what is so close in time should now have so remote a feeling. It was a time of change. There was a more dramatic transformation in lifestyle for most Britons than any other decade this century. At the start, wartime rationing of food and other staples was still widespread, the Berlin Airlift had only just been concluded and the Korean war was in full swing with British and Commonwealth forces heavily involved. By the end, Prime Minister Harold Macmillan was telling the country 'You've never had it so good,' and he reduced income tax to prove it. There were grumbles because petrol cost three shillings a gallon. Identity Cards were abolished. The Coronation of Queen Elizabeth II was a glittering occasion and the first sign of the diminution of post-war austerity. The news that Hillary and Tensing had finally conquered Mount Everest added to the general euphoria. Gordon Richards won his first Derby. Bannister shattered the 4-minute-mile barrier. Unemployment stood at 620,728. Parking-meters appeared in London. Speedsters were checked by radar-traps. The sinking of the Oxford boat caused the Boat Race to be cancelled. The first test explosion of the British atom bomb took place off the coast of Australia. Pictures from a Soviet spacecraft revealed the first-ever glimpse of the dark side of the moon. Earthbound golfers spurned luxury travel when the team crossed the Atlantic in the *Queen Mary*. Cabin class instead of first class tickets produced a saving of approximately £1,250.

Golfing happenings recall headlines now forgotten. The American Government proposed that the rearmament drive could be helped by golfers. The Treasury Secretary suggested that a twenty-per-cent tax on all green fees would increase revenue by £3,500,000. Stake money for the British tournament season amounted to £25,000, the maximum prize being a possible £5,250, a figure earned by the 30th placing in the 1990 Open Championship. The death of the Reverend Harcourt Just at the age of ninety-four meant only one man was left entitled to golf free on the Old Course, St Andrews. He was the first golfer to qualify for the concession open to any local golfer attaining ninety years. Mr Cheape then became the only man entitled to such free golf. His rights were traced to the Links Act of 1894. His father sold to St Andrews the land on which the links are laid out. A different type of record took place on the Addington course. Two club golfers had a bet of 1,000 guineas that the round could not be completed in under 750 strokes. The usual golf ball was not used: instead a plastic ball weighing roughly a quarter-of-an-ounce was substituted. The winner of the bet completed the eighteen holes in 409 strokes. He needed 57 at his worst hole and 13 at his best. More noteworthy was the defeat of Oxford University 12–6 over the Sunningdale women's course by a team of women golfers. The same team lost to Brigadier Critchley's side by 15–3. The weaker sex had one consolation. Colonel H. Nugent-Head, a noted long hitter, declared that no woman could beat him on any course playing level. He played Frances Stephens and lost 3 and 2.

Items such as these seem trivial against the broad background of the history of the game, yet each mirrors something of the flavour of the era, landmarks that put things in a time-perspective. J. H. Taylor, five times Open Champion, attained his eightieth birthday. Francis Ouimet announced he had taken part in his last Walker Cup match, closing an extraordinary innings that began in the 1921 unofficial match. Ben Hogan won the American Open Championship for the third time. Max Faulkner completed the double when he added the title of Master Golfer to that of Open Champion. John Panton, after only two seasons in tournament golf, headed the Order of Merit table and won the Harry Vardon Trophy. He averaged 71.51 strokes for 37 tournament rounds. Lloyd Mangrum ousted Sam Snead as top money-spinner in American golf with earnings of £93,000 the lowest total since 1942. Mangrum averaged 70.05 per round in 104 tournament rounds. Ben Hogan was named Golfer of the Year for the third time by American sports writers.

The English Championship was decided at the thirty-ninth hole at Hunstanton by a stymie. The winner, Geoffrey Roberts of Southport and Ainsdale, had been 3 down at the end of the first round. A few months later the stymie officially disappeared. At the same time the centre-shafted putter was declared a legal weapon. Max Faulkner added ten inches of wood to an ordinary putter. The result was a club longer (44 inches) than his driver. The shaft touched his chest when putting. It worked like a dream – at least for a time. Babe Zaharias lopped three shots off the women's world record for four rounds. Figures of 71–70–74–73 ... 288 won the Tampa Women's Open Tournament. Tom Haliburton, the Wentworth professional, went round the 6,375-yard Worthing course in 61 strokes, the lowest round at that time returned in a British professional tournament. Proposals were put forward that the University Match should always be played on the same course. Rye was suggested. It is interesting to recall the ranking list of amateur golfers issued by the English Golf Union. It was their first list of revised handicaps under the new Standard Scratch Score scheme. Ronnie White headed the table on plus-two. Seventeen other players were given a plus-one rating. They were Ian Caldwell, L. G. Crawley, J. W. Jones, J. D. A. Langley, M. Lee, P. B. Lucas, D. H. R. Martin, G. H. Micklem, J. Payne, A. H. Perowne, D. Rawlinson, P. F. Scrutton, C. Stowe, Robert Sweeny, K. H. Thom, C. J. H. Tolley and S. V. Tredinnick. There are many famous names in the list, little known maybe by the current generation but who at their peak reflected amateur golf at its best.

Two items at the time made golfing headlines. Under the rule that prevented members demonstrating golf or acting as salesmen in sports shops, the Professional Golfers' Association suspended Bob McKenzie, their outgoing chairman, founder member and honorary life member. The suspension was due to McKenzie working for several months in a London West End store where golf equipment was sold. The United States Golf Association announced the development of a new type of divot-proof grass. It was weed-free and required no watering. It was predicted that the 5,000 golf clubs scattered throughout America would save something like £45,000,000 on course maintenance. Dr Frank Drau, director of the Association's Green Section, predicted there would be no clover and everyone would have a brassy lie ... if only it was true.

The Stranahan Phenomenon

Finally, there was an item of news that Frank Stranahan, American holder of the British Amateur Championship, had won the Ohio light-heavyweight weightlifting title by raising 725 lb in three lifts. I single out

Frank for here was an American who made his mark on both sides of the Atlantic as an amateur golfer of outstanding qualities. He set a personal standard of near-perfection. Writers who tried to produce an accurate pen-portrait experienced difficulty. At first contact he seemed a straightforward subject until an attempt was made to find what lay behind the facade he showed to the world. Stranahan for several years was the most interesting personality in world amateur golf. An individualist in every sense of the word, Stranahan was the lone wolf of the fairways. Few golfers have attempted to subject themselves to such concentrated self-discipline. His ambition was to become the greatest shot-maker relying on total co-ordination of mind and muscle. No one could question the thoroughness of his approach. Technique was analysed in every detail. The only thing missing was ability to eliminate error. Back-breaking, hand-blistering hours spent practising and experimenting could do nothing about it. I watched him during his triumphant progress in the British Amateur. Charles Stowe fell to him at Sandwich by 5 and 4 in a final that is remembered by contrasting styles. Stowe showed glimpses of the slashing methods of Alfred Perry but was unable to cope with automaton-like consistency. At St Andrews in 1950 the finalists were both American. Richard Chapman had the zest of an enthusiast, but could not match Stranahan's pin-point accuracy. The margin was 8 and 6. Afterwards I joined him in a small private dinner party in Lundin Links hotel, happy to escape the attention of pressmen. The relationship was not always happy. He was indifferent to criticism, ignored public comment and inac-curate journalese. He pursued his self-appointed course of endless practice, both on and off the course. I remember him saying that of all London hotels, his favourite was Claridge's, not on the grounds of luxury, food or service, but because of the carpeting in the suites. Texture and pile were ideal for putting. Back would be pushed the furniture and conversation continued as he paced up and down, putter in hand. I liked and admired Frank Stranahan. His enthusiasm has not been matched. It acted like a tonic and exercised considerable influence on the amateur game. Golf was poorer when he retired.

Invigorating Joe Carr

Other golfers who hit the headlines were Joe Carr, whose charismatic Irish charm hid a resolute golfer capable of sustained concentration. His Amateur successes were achieved against Harvie Ward at Hoylake by

2 holes; Alan Thirlwell by 3 and 2 on the Old Course, and R. Cochran of America by 8 and 7 at Portrush. Carr's style repaid study. He had the reputation of being a lusty hitter achieved with unorthodox method and quick swing. The power of forearms and wrists produced the results, although woods were inclined to be erratic. He then decided to remodel his style. Gone was the heart-warming slashing style. The swing was lengthened with gratifying results as regards accuracy.

Commonwealth Domination

This decade saw the previous American monopoly of the Open Championship succeeded by Commonwealth domination. Bobby Locke of South Africa won the title four times, though at Sandwich fortune smiled on him. He tied with Harry Bradshaw, a cheerful Irishman with a style decidedly unorthodox. At times he held the club the reverse way. The right hand came at the top of the shaft, a habit inherited from the days when he played hurling. He argued convincingly that the reverse grip is the quickest way to ensure a straight left arm in the backswing. The switch to orthodox methods was not natural. It felt awkward and clumsy. Eventually a compromise produced a grip with the last three fingers of the right hand taken off the shaft and overlapping the left. Alongside Locke the contrast in style was marked. It was not until the episode with a bottle, when the Irishman found his ball had rolled inside, that the scales finally tipped in the South African's favour. More impressive was Locke's win over Roberto de Vicenzo in 1950 by two strokes. On the other two occasions when he won the Open, Peter Thomson was the victim. Locke first played in this country as a slim amateur, an outline that changed with the years. My memory is of a rotund figure in plus-fours and large white cap striding triumphantly down the last fairway of the Old Course in 1957. As an individual Locke was not everybody's choice, somewhat argumentative and prickly, but there was no doubting his status in world ranking.

Peter Thomson was not so aggressive; for an Australian, he was surprisingly mild with quiet good humour that showed golf was primarily a game to be enjoyed. His enthusiasm never waned. Such was his success it was the rest of the field who looked glum with good reason. For some eight years he monopolized the Open to such an extent that the only doubt was the identity of the runner-up. He took that place on three occasions; the other five saw him walk off with the trophy. It was a similar story in New Zealand and Australia. Thomson had the rare knack of making shot-making look effortless. He was the orthodox machine. Instead of retiring, Thomson found a new lease of life collecting substantial cheques on the Veteran's tournament circuit, rewards far in excess of winnings in his prime, such are the advantages of inflation.

The chain of overseas wins was broken by that extrovert peacock Max Faulkner. His belief in himself was remarkable. At Portrush after the second round of the Open, he is said to have signed autographs as the Open Champion. The story could well be true, for it became fact and silenced those of a superstitious nature who felt such cockiness asked for trouble. It never happened. Max lacked the natural showmanship of Walter Hagen and Jimmy Demaret, but is remembered as an agreeable clown and a determined competitive professional. I suppose his son-in-law, Brian Barnes, tried to follow in his footsteps, but pale copies are never as appealing as the original. Another professional to hit the headlines for aggressive posings was Norman von Nida, a tough, half-pint-sized Australian who always had a chip on his shoulder. He was a rare omelette of a man, at times pleasant and approachable, then, in a flash, argumentative, if not abusive, yet underneath this traditional tough guise was an agreeable fellow who was afraid that pleasantries might be interpreted as softness. Australians are a law unto themselves when it comes to behaviour patterns. It was a pity, for Norman was a fine golfer. He returned to this country years later, bespectacled and benign. No one who met him could imagine what he was once like. It seemed unnatural. He was nicer when he was nastier because no one believed in his belligerence. He would have made a newsworthy Open Champion.

Kel Nagle was quite different, in fact unique. Whoever heard of an unassuming Australian? History remembers him as a worthy winner of the Centenary Open Championship at St Andrews. There have been many exciting finishes to the Open, but few have equalled the tenseness of that final round in the three-cornered battle between Arnold Palmer, then American champion, Roberto de Vicenzo, and Kel Nagle. The American was favourite, his greater experience was expected to tip the scales, but in the end it was the Australian who stood on the eighteenth green needing two shots to win from three feet. Even at the moment of his greatest success, Nagle paid tribute to his fellow countryman, Peter Thomson, for all the assistance he had given him, including a tactical coaching round on the Old Course. He was certainly a receptive pupil. His tribute typified the man. On the links Kel Nagle is remembered as an admirable ambassador for his country.

Max Faulkner, always a colourful, extrovert performer whose belief in himself affected many an opponent, even to the extent of signing autographs as the Open Champion when he finished his second round at Portrush. His confidence was justified. He broke the chain of overseas wins in the Open.

The place of Kel Nagle in golfing history was assured when he won the Centenary Open Championship on the Old Course. He was an admirable ambassador for his country.

The American professional scene produced several outstanding players who left their mark on the game. Billy Casper had won the 1959 United States Open at Mamaroneck, a popular success for he was twice nominated Player of the Year and had three times been recipient of the Byron Nelson Award. Julius Boros demonstrated at Dallas in 1952 that the title could be won with a delicacy of touch that belied his rugged appearance. Ed Furgol was an unexpected winner in 1954 when he did so in spite of a physical disability that would have side-lined many players. A withered and locked left arm meant adapting his game into a right-hand action, helped by making the left-hand grip as thick as a tennis racquet handle with the right thumb on the side of the shaft. The style made a nonsense of the straight left-arm theory. It worked and theorists were silenced. Arnold Palmer and Jack Nicklaus had broken through. Palmer collected the 1954 Amateur title at Detroit; Nicklaus followed suit five years later at Broadmoor. Sam Snead was still trying to win the elusive United States Open. Even a double Masters title did not compensate. The decade closed with Gary Player becoming the first overseas player to win the American Open for 45 years. The little South African demonstrated how a half-pint-sized could take on opponents far more powerful. At 5 feet 7 inches tall and scaling some 150 pounds, he outdrove the big boys and attributed his physical fitness to a rigid training schedule that kept him at peak level.

Two women golfers were outstanding in this country. Mrs George Valentine, perhaps better known as Jessie Anderson, was awarded an MBE in the 1959 Honours List for 'Services to golf', the first woman golfer to receive such recognition. Her success was remarkable. The tally included three British, six Scottish, French and New Zealand titles. She was the only golfer to win the British Championship before and after the war, in 1937, repeated in 1955 and 1958, and runner-up in 1950 and 1957. Wee Jessie personified consistency, a worthy member of the Andersons of Perth, whose contributions to the game take us back to the heyday of the Morrises. Equally outstanding was Mrs Frances Smith, again more familiar to some by her maiden name of 'Bunty' Smith. Coached by her father, Fred Stephens, professional at Bootle Golf Club, Liverpool, she pursued a training schedule that left her with exceptionally strong hands and fingers. She had an unusual feature in her style that other women golfers might copy to advantage. There was a pronounced pause at the top of the backswing, part of a routine that never varied. It produced precision golf. As an extra I add the name of Vicomtesse de Saint Sauveur, daughter of a famous French golfing family, who, as Lally Vagliano, played for France

Arnold Palmer's style was free and flowing like his swing. He was in a category of his own. Who can forget the scenes as 'Arnie's Army' swept across the fairways in support of their man. It is hard to express his influence on the game to anyone who has not felt the impact of his personality.

Close-up shots by television cameras have frozen tense moments under terrific pressures. No other golfer reflects so truly the tremendous concentration needed in the closing stages of a championship as Jack Nicklaus. The sense of awareness almost etches itself on the screen. Jack is the supreme example of how golf should be played when the stakes are great.

Frances 'Bunty' Stephens had a brilliant international career in which she lost not a single match and was twice lady champion in 1949 and 1954. She was awarded the OBE for Services to golf and was president of the English Ladies Golf Association at the time of her death in 1978. She maintained that under normal conditions all ladies' courses were too short.

at the age of sixteen, added the Girls' Championship the same season, and the British title at Newcastle, Co. Down, in 1950. In all, she won 20 national championships and gave heart to many women that it is possible to be feminine and pretty whilst producing ruthless, aggressive golf.

Muirfield Reminiscences

I have left to the last the two outstanding features of the Fifties, but before so doing I have singled out one of the championship links that featured prominently in the decade. It was the scene of the 1959 Open Championship when Gary Player burst on the winner's board. No more historic ground could be found for Muirfield is one of the oldest golf clubs in the world. The claim that the Honourable Company of Edinburgh Golfers is the senior of all clubs is substantiated by trustworthy evidence. Blackheath is said to have been founded in 1608, but there are doubts about the accuracy of the date, whilst Royal Burgess maintains it was a golfing society in 1735, but again the evidence is not conclusive. There is nothing hearsay about the written proof confirming the existence of the Gentlemen Golfers of Leith in 1744, which is ten years earlier than the beginnings of the Royal and Ancient Club.

The Gentlemen Golfers moved from Leith to Musselburgh, finally transferring to Muirfield in 1891 as the Honourable Company of Edinburgh Golfers. The course was not regarded as genuine links-land. It was only 5,280 yards long and enclosed by a wall. Modifications removed the seaward wall, incorporated a magnificent stretch of rolling sand-dunes and extended the length to some 7,000 yards of natural seaside turf. The clubhouse mirrors what a nineteenth of tradition should look like. The tendency today is to ape the appearance and facilities of a Hilton hotel, particularly in America. Muirfield reflects its historic role. It was here, more than two centuries ago, that the first set of rules of the game were drawn up by John Rattray, an Edinburgh surgeon and former Captain of the Golf. This same gentleman was instructed by Charles Edward Stuart to look after his troops during their invasion of England and had to be rescued by Duncan Forbes of Culloden, also a Gentleman Golfer and one-time Secretary of the club.

But all that is a long time ago. Since then much has happened on its links. The first Open Championship was held at Muirfield in 1892, the year when the old tournament of thirty-six holes was exchanged for four rounds of eighteen holes. The previous year Hugh Kirkaldy had won the

Diana Fishwick, winner of the Ladies Championship at Formby in 1930 with Glenna Collett Vare, America's greatest woman golfer, who raised the standard for her fellow countrywomen.

title with a score of 166, beating in the process, with his brother Andrew, the St Andrews course record of 77 set up the year before by young Tom Morris. Hugh's outward half of 33 strokes on the Old Course was a remarkable feat. The Kirkaldys could not repeat the performance at Muirfield. To make matters worse for the Scottish professionals, the title went not only to an amateur but an Englishman in Harold Hilton. Small wonder that Andrew Kirkaldy described Muirfield as 'an auld water meadie'.

Early rounds did not suggest that Hilton would win. Little went right in the first thirty-six holes and he finished eight shots behind the leader. Fortunes changed when he almost holed out for one at the short first in the third round. He went on to break the course record with a 72 and lunched only three strokes behind. The final round began shakily with a four and a six, he holed two pitch shots for birdies, finishing in 74 to win the Championship by three shots with an aggregate of 305. Critics at the time said Hilton was lucky, but he refuted the charge by adding a second Open title, three Amateur Championships and an American Amateur win.

Four years later the Open returned to Muirfield. It produced a straight duel between Harry Vardon and J. H. Taylor. Had the latter won, it would have been his third consecutive victory, later achieved by Ferguson at Musselburgh, Prestwick and St Andrews in 1880–2. The Open was still a two-day affair; thirty-six holes each day. At the halfway stage Taylor led from Vardon. The final is described in Vardon's dated words:

> On the second day it so happened that J. H. was playing a few holes ahead of me. Late in the contest it became apparent that the issue would be decided in favour of one of us. Three or four holes from the finish I was told how many strokes were still left for me to play if I were to win. When I arrived at the last tee, I was set with an extremely difficult problem. I required a four to gain a victory outright and a five to tie, which would give me the right to play-off with him for the Championship. The last hole at Muirfield at this period was a testing one, requiring as it did a good drive and a real good brassie to reach the green. There was, however, a bunker guarding the green, and while there was very little difficulty in securing the necessary five to tie, I might easily take a six in attempting to reach the green with my second. After hitting a good tee-shot the temptation to have a go for the green with my brassie was strong. The decision was affected by a friend, James Kay of Seaton Carew, pointing to the ground this side of the bunker. I played short, holed out in five and tied with Taylor on 316.

The play-off was impossible next day as both men were playing in a tournament at North Berwick, but play resumed on the Saturday morning. Vardon finished the first eighteen holes with a lead of two strokes. After lunch he went on to win by four shots, the first of Vardon's six Open Championship wins. Shot-making may have changed, and scoring made to look easier, but the tensions were the same.

Five years later it was James Braid's turn. At the end of the first day's play, the triumvirate domination was clear:

James Braid	. . . . . .	155
Harry Vardon	. . . . .	155
J. H. Taylor	. . . . . .	162

Here was the forerunner of the Palmer-Player-Nicklaus monopoly. Braid had been plagued with putting jitters and came to Muirfield with an aluminium putter which worked wonders. Seventy-three in the third round gave him a lead of six strokes over Vardon. In the final round the margin was reduced to three shots as the aluminium wand stuttered, but Braid held on to win by a margin of four strokes. The Open at Muirfield was the end of an era, for in 1902 the new rubber-cored ball was introduced. Sandy Herd played with it to win the title at Hoylake.

In 1906 Braid recorded his third victory in the Open at Muirfield. He defended his title in faultless fashion, needing a final round of 76 to win as the two nearest contenders, Taylor and Vardon, had finished early. Braid's tee-shot in the last round had a Ballesteros touch as it finished on the second tee. He got his par 3, went out in 38, carding the inward half in eight pars and one birdie. He finished with an aggregate of 300 and victory by four strokes. Once again it had been a triumvirate picnic claiming the first three places.

Muirfield, 1912, was Ted Ray's year. Bernard Darwin described this granite golfer as a man 'whom Nyren might have called, as did Tom Walker, "that anointed clod-stumper"'. With rough-hewn strength, something of a bucolic air, and a swing unpolished and unorthodox but having the saving grace of rhythm, Ray combined a delicate touch in the short game. He was unquestionably the player of his year and always a formidable one, not to be judged by any too-nice and pedantic standards. He was a 'character' with devastating powers of recovery, and a cartoonist's dream with distinctive clothing and inevitable pipe, in many ways the predecessor of Lee Trevino. There was no doubt about his win at Muirfield. He led every round and had the luxury of a five-stroke lead when the final eighteen holes began. For once he played within his usual game. Spectacular effects were resisted and he cruised home in unruffled style. His pipe-drill eased many a putt. At a critical point he would have a refill

Gary Player, a diminutive golfer who outdrives opponents far more powerful. Now playing in veterans' tournaments, the South African retains his peak of physical fitness by a rigid training schedule.

Moments to savour. Dai Rees at Lindrick after winning the Ryder Cup match against America.

and steady his nerves. I imagine he became Brian Barnes' model.

Seventeen years passed before the Championship returned to Muirfield. By then the trophy had virtually become American property. Season after season their invasion was successful, and 1929 was no exception. The previous season Walter Hagen had won his third Championship and received the trophy from the Prince of Wales. This time he had to overcome a strong entry, plus appalling weather conditions. High winds swept across the exposed links. His performance belied a reputation of being a fair-weather golfer. The American contingent swept the board. Only Abe Mitchell and Percy Alliss, father of the BBC commentator, put up any sort of opposition. There were 242 entries. Ninety-five professionals and fourteen amateurs qualified. The total was reduced to fifty-eight pro-fessionals and six amateurs for the last thirty-six holes. This was to be Hagen's fourth and last win in the Open, certainly the most colourful victor seen at Muirfield. The first ten finishers of that final round gave some indication of American supremacy:

Walter Hagen (USA)	75–67–75–75 – 292
Johnny Farrell (USA)	72–75–76–75 – 298
Leo Diegel (USA)	71–69–82–77 – 299
Abe Mitchell (St Albans)	72–72–78–78 – 300
Percy Alliss (Berlin)	69–76–76–79 – 300
Robert Cruickshank (USA)	73–74–78–76 – 301
Jim Barnes (USA)	71–80–78–74 – 303
Al Watrous (USA)	73–79–75–77 – 304
Gene Sarazen (USA)	73–74–81–76 – 304
Tommy Armour (USA)	75–73–79–78 – 305

Muirfield produced a surprise result in 1935. Henry Cotton was the pre-Championship favourite. Nobody seriously considered the chances of Alfred Perry. He just missed the qualifying cut by one shot, thankful to be bracketed in the lowly seventy-third slot. But when the action started Perry returned an unexpected 69 which Cotton bettered by one shot. He needed a four for 66, but visits to two bunkers meant a six. Padgham and Charles Whitcombe applied pressure in the second rounds with 72 and 68 against Perry's 75. Cotton returned 74. In the third round Perry equalled Hagen's record of 67 and led by a single stroke from Whitcombe. In the last round Perry indulged in a whirlwind exhibition of slashing, rumbustious golf. He took every kind of gamble, such as wielding a spoon from a bunker. In the end he triumphed by four shots with a total of 283.

That refreshing breath of carefree golf was repeated in more serious vein in 1948. This time Cotton gained his third Open victory. In 1934 he had halted the American rash of wins with a memorable success at Sandwich. In 1937 he repeated the win at Carnoustie against the full might of the American Ryder Cup team. At Muirfield he mastered the narrow fairways and tiger rough to win by five strokes from Fred Daly. His second round was played before King George VI. It was near perfection. The card deserves to be remembered:

Out: 3-4-5-3-4-4-3-4-3—33
In: 4-4-4-3-4-3-3-4-4—33—66

1959 produced a tension-laden final day that centred round Gary Player. At the outset of the Championship, the South African found Muirfield a difficult test. The first round of 75 did little for his chances. Two rounds completed and he trailed the leader by eight shots. The third round included an inward half of 33 for 71. The gap was now four strokes. The final round saw Player at his best. Out in 34 he reached the eighteenth tee needing 4 for 66 to equal the course record. The title was in sight, but a bunkered drive meant just reaching the green in three shots. He three-putted for a six. Sixty-eight and an aggregate of 284 was good but by no means certain. Unlike the present method that brackets the leading players together, the nearest contenders were a long way behind. It was nearly two hours before the South African gained his first Open title by two shots in the last Open of the decade.

The Lindrick Miracle

October 5th, 1957, was a day to savour. The location was Lindrick Golf Club; occasion, the Ryder Cup match against the United States in which Great Britain, denied victory for twenty-three years, were the under-dogs. Everything suggested another defeat with a deficit of 1–3 in the foursomes, the opening day being marred by dissension among the British team and complaints from the Americans that the arrangements for their comfort left much to be desired. That proud moment at Southport in 1933 when Syd Easterbrook sank a trick putt on the last match of the last green to give Britain victory seemed light years away. It was matched by the traumatic happenings at Lindrick. A stiffening breeze made the gorse-lined fairways more demanding, strong enough to prevent the strict professional par of 69 being bettered. Britain attacked straight away, took early leads and clung on to them. Mills, regarded by some as out of his depth, confounded critics by beating the American captain, Jack Burke, 5 and 3. Ken Bousfield, 71 against 76, had the measure of Lionel Herbert. Bernard Hunt downed Doug Ford 6 and 5. Christy O'Connor, the matchplay champion, all square against Doug Finsterwald, turned on the heat after lunch with 4–4–3–4–4–3–4–3 to win 7 and 6. Dick Mayer, the American Open champion, went into lunch 1 up against Harry Bradshaw, but the Irishman's 71 produced a half. Dai Rees, an inspiring captain, beat Ed Furgol 7 and 6. Eric Brown, matched against an equally dynamic personality in Tommy Bolt, had the satisfaction of beating a volatile opponent who lived up to his reputation by fracturing his club by thumping the ground in frustration. Only Peter Alliss bit the dust 2 and 1 against Fred Hawkins.

It was an unforgettable day made possible by the dynamic leadership of Dai Rees. His sheer enthusiasm inspired his men. Team spirit powered the way to victory, proving yet again that belief in oneself can work miracles. Lindrick was little short of miraculous. It was the tonic that dispelled the myth of American invincibility.

Foursomes

Great Britain		United States of America	
P. Alliss & B. J. Hunt . . .	0	D. Ford & D. Finsterwald (2 & 1)	1
K. Bousfield & D. J. Rees (3 & 2)	1	A. Wall & F. Hawkins . . .	0
M. Faulkner & H. Weetman	0	T. Kroll & J. Burke	1
C. O'Connor & E. C. Brown .	0	R. Mayer & T. Bolt (7 & 5) .	1
	1		3

Singles

E.C. Brown (4 & 3)	1	T. Bolt	0
R.P. Mills (5 & 3).	1	J. Burke	0
P. Alliss	0	F. Hawkins (2 & 1)	1
K. Bousfield (4 & 3)	1	L. Herbert	0
D.J. Rees (7 & 6)	1	E. Furgol	0
B.J. Hunt (6 & 5).	1	D. Ford	0
C. O'Connor (7 & 6). . . .	1	D. Finsterwald	0
H. Bradshaw (halved) . . .	0	R. Mayer (halved)	0
	6		1

Grand Aggregate: Great Britain, 7 matches: USA 4 matches, 1 halved.
Captains: Dai Rees, Great Britain; Jack Burke, USA.

15

The Golf Machine Called
Ben Hogan

BEN HOGAN attained a peak of perfection in his mastery of shot-making that has not been surpassed. In 1948 he won eleven tournaments including the United States Open Championship with an all-time low of 276 and a second PGA title. Everything was set fair for domination of the golfing scene when a near-fatal accident, a head-on crash with a lorry in the fog, threatened to terminate his playing career in 1949. Recovery was miraculous. Later that year he came to England as non-playing captain of the American Ryder Cup team. At Southampton a fleet of Bentleys waited to take the party to the Savoy Hotel in London. I sat with Ben and Valerie in the first car, but it soon showed that his nerves were on edge. The memory of the crash and the fact that oncoming traffic seemed to be on the wrong side of the road caused such tension that I suggested dropping back in the car-cavalcade and reducing speed. The next morning, Ben had recovered his poise and we went by road to Scarborough via Oxford where the team had coffee with the Fellows of Christ Church, then on to Stratford-upon-Avon for an official lunch.

In spite of being in constant pain and virtually encased in a rubber suit, Hogan led his team to a close victory. On returning to the States, grim determination brought him back to the tournament circuit, not token appearances, but victory in three National Championships in 1953. He finished first in the five events entered, including his second Masters Tournament, the fourth American Championship, and the Open Championship at his first attempt, plus a third PGA title. The extent of his recovery was a tribute to incredible recuperative powers.

Watching Ben Hogan in action was a visual insight into his tempera-

Names to remember, a
different generation of
American professionals.
Left to right, back row:
Lloyd Mangrum, Clayton
Heafner, Ed Dudley, Sam
Snead, Johnny Palmer;
front row: Skip
Alexander, Jimmy
Demaret, Ben Hogan,
Chick Harbert, Dutch
Harrison.

The legend himself ...
Ben Hogan.

ment, a psychological experience. The last day of an Open Championship is a tremendous strain on any man with a chance of winning. The third round is critical, but nothing tests nerve and stamina like the final nine holes. Every champion has his own fingerprints of style and mannerisms and these are on show during the closing stages. I think of the placid demeanour of Bobby Jones at Hoylake in 1930, the lordly gait of Walter Hagen the year before, the grin of Gene Sarazen at Prince's in 1932, the strained expression of Henry Cotton at Carnoustie two years later, whistling Fred Daly, the magnitude of Bobby Locke, slamming Sam Snead at St Andrews, and so on. Ben Hogan was something new. Cotton earned the sobriquet 'Concentration Henry', but for ice-cold detachment Hogan made Cotton appear light-hearted.

Throughout the excitement and turmoil of that last round, Hogan looked the coolest of the milling galleries. At that time spectators had more freedom of movement. He smoked cigarettes with poker-faced composure. On the train to Scotland I re-read Hogan's book *Power Golf*. I was reminded of an extract from Ed Dudley's foreword:

During the war Bobby Jones played with Hogan in a big tournament in Chicago. Afterwards he told Grantland Rice, who told me, 'I thought I was a hard worker at the game. I thought Hagen and Sarazen were hard workers. But Ben Hogan is the hardest worker I've ever known, not only in golf, but in any other sport. I've taken my share of beatings, so have all the others. But no one has ever taken the beatings Hogan takes. He thinks only in terms of birdies. Several times out there he was actually trying to hole out a sixty- or seventy-yard pitch. His goal is never the green. It's the cup. And you can say that ability to take punishment is a big part of winning golf!'

Every word was true. Never had I seen such calculating shot-making. Locke had a reputation for microscopic examination of every blade of grass before putting. Alongside Hogan's shot-preparation, the South African seemed positively careless. When Hogan studied the line of a putt you felt the ball was bound to drop. I have used the phrase 'looking at the ball intelligently'. Here it was seen in practice.

Every final round in a successful championship bid has one or two vital shots that turned the scales. Hogan was no exception in Carnoustie. He was fortunate at the fifth missing a bunker by a lucky break, then sank a 20-yard chip for a birdie 3. The let-off was followed by a useful 4 at the controversial 567-yard sixth. Two at the thirteenth was the reward for a

15-foot putt. The sixteenth can be baffling. Snead disliked it in 1937, but it held no terrors for Hogan. Down went a par 3. The record-breaking round of 68 was copybook golf.

When Provost William McLaughlan presented the trophy to Hogan, I recalled the scene sixteen years earlier when the award went to Henry Cotton. The evening was damp after a frightful day of incessant wind and rain. James Wright made the presentation with a few remarks eulogizing the virtues of Carnoustie. There was Ed Dudley, the leading American with a full head of hair, Walter Hagen, figure still streamlined, and Henry Cotton, even younger looking than his years. That day we hailed a great home victory against powerful opposition. Now it was the turn to applaud Ben Hogan's memorable win, the finest since the heyday of Bobby Jones.

Hogan in Defeat

I think of the 1955 United States Open, a championship that produced a sensational result. The setting itself was memorable. San Francisco with its cable cars and sidewalk flower stands, of North Beach, the Redwoods, Ocean Beach, Seal Rocks, and the vast bay with its Golden Gate, each spanned by one of the world's two greatest bridges; then the Olympic Golf Club at Lakeside, laid out by the Pacific, venue of the championship. All the ingredients were there. The course set a tough examination. Critics declared that more golf balls were lost in this Open than any ten previous events. When a professional waded into the thick rough there was always the chance of flushing out a caddie or two. Robert Trent Jones, the golf course architect, kept a check on the length of drives. The average length of the lustiest hitters in the four rounds was 216 yards, the average roll on all tee shots being under 10 yards. The rough lived up to its name. A perennial rye of a kind not previously found on an Open links proved more punishing than had been anticipated. Being allowed to grow too long, it over-encroached the fairways and around the greens. Large quantities of *Poa annua* grass on the greens made them difficult to read. Many professionals complained the greens were too small. Lay-out measured 6,700 yards, but under existing conditions it played longer than 7,000 yards.

Regarding the players, pride of place had to go to the unknown Jack Fleck, the man who staged one of the most dramatic finishes in the history of championship golf. Ben Hogan had completed his round in confident fashion. His reception from the huge crowd round the home green was inspiring. Gene Sarazen had rushed across with a hand-microphone. Radio listeners heard Hogan described as the only man to win five National Open Championships. I took a photograph showing him holding up an outspread right hand, five fingers symbolizing the feat, offered congratulations and repeated the praise to Valerie Hogan about ten minutes later in the clubhouse. News seeped through that a 1,000–1 outsider had a remote chance, possibly of tieing. Fleck was roughly two hours behind Hogan. It seemed an eternity, but figures kept the hope alive. At last Fleck stood on the final tee. A hooked drive found the rough. That was that. A wonderful effort, but surely Hogan had the title in the bag. We underestimated the 'unknown'. A magnificent recovery just reached the green. I asked him afterwards what had been his reaction. Recollection was vague, but one thought was uppermost. He had to swing the club without over-forcing. He succeeded. Rarely have I seen a finer recovery under such mental pressure. The putt, some thirty feet, must have looked a mile. Without a sign of nerves, Fleck studied the line, struck the ball calmly as though only a dollar was at stake. It dropped into the hole. Fleck raised both arms, swayed and looked as if he would collapse. Police escorted him to the official tent. Fleck was literally speechless, played out on his feet. Reaction set in. The first to appreciate it was the defending champion, Ed Furgol, who had just seen his title disappear. He took Fleck under his care, led him to the locker-room, saw that he rested, went with him to the pressroom and gave the answers that were wanted. Furgol's only comment was that he had been in a similar position himself the year before and knew something of Fleck's mental turmoil.

The play-off was expected to be one-sided. I thought Hogan would turn on the pressure and run out winner by five or six shots. I couldn't have been more wrong. Fleck shot 69, one under par. Hogan carded 72. The end came at the eighteenth. Hogan pulled the tee-shot into the hillside rough. Fleck played safely down the middle with his spoon. Hogan was ankle-deep. He swung, scythe-like, but only lush grass came up. He swung again. The ball shifted a couple of feet. The green was only 130 yards away, but still Hogan had to aim for safety with a sideways shot. This time he had made it. Fleck was on in 2, Hogan forty feet away in 5. To his credit Hogan sank the massive putt for 6. Fleck left the putt near enough to make the next one a mere formality. It gave him 6,000 dollars, his first tournament victory and the National crown.

So ended Hogan's bid to stand alone in the record-books above Bobby Jones and Willie Anderson, who had both won four. At the presentation Fleck sat in a daze. He was the unknown golfer who dreamt he had won the US Open and found it was true. His speech was short but sincere. Later that night I dined at Trader Vic's on Fishermen's Wharf with Ben and Valerie Hogan and Bing Crosby. It had been an unusual experience for Ben to lose in such a fashion. It is easy to be magnanimous to a defeated opponent, but quite a different matter when a great ambition has been snatched away. His praise of Fleck was spontaneous and genuine. In no way did he seek to detract from his success. I can only say that in defeat Ben Hogan was a generous loser without a trace of envy, the mark of a true sportsman.

The Verdict

Ben Hogan had that intangible quality we call genius. The methods he used have not dated. The Spanish have a word *duende*. It has no exact English equivalent, but it denotes the quality without which no flamenco singer or bull-fighter can conquer the summit of his art. The ability to transmit a profoundly felt emotion to an audience or gallery of strangers with the minimum of fuss and the maximum of restraint. That is as near as our language can come to the full meaning of *duende*. Ben Hogan had it in rich measure. Certainly nobody has ever compared him with his imitators. He remains the legend. Hogan and Jack Nicklaus, are the two finest golfers the game has known, exercising immense influence in their time.

16

The Phenomenon of James Bruen

THE Amateur Championship was an indicator of current top-line form for many years, but between the wars the title almost became an American monopoly. On the few occasions when home players won, credit must go to the fighting golf of such Irishmen as Joe Carr, Sam McCready and James Bruen. The broad tradition of the game was enriched by the welcome revival of Irish golf at international level, with contributions by the likes of H. M. Cairnes, Lionel Munn, Charles Hezlet, J. D. McCormack, D. E. B. Soulby, John Burke, Cecil Ewing, J. C. Brown, and so on. For special mention I choose James Bruen. The first time I saw him play was in the Boys' Championship at Birkdale in 1936. He made mincemeat of the opposition that week, in the final overwhelming young Innes by 11 and 9. When success comes too early there is often a tendency to become over-conscious of prowess. For that reason it was perhaps just as well that Bruen did not get far in his first Amateur Championship.

Bruen was then seventeen years of age. His opponent, Richard Chapman, had no mercy. A turbulent second-round match put the Irish lad on the side-lines. That somewhat inauspicious entry into major cham-pionship golf had been preceded by two excellent performances. Bruen finished second in both the St George's Cup and the Prince of Wales Cup, being defeated by such experienced men as D. H. R. Martin and Charles Stowe. There, at least, was a hint of the potential.

The following season saw the promise come to fruition in the Walker Cup trial matches at St Andrews. I had lively respect for Bobby Jones' record-total aggregate of 285 in the 1927 Open Championship. Conse-quently it came as a surprise when the eighteen-year-old youngster played nine rounds over the Old Course and only once needed more than 71. The first round was 68. The next three cards beat Jones's record by a couple of shots. Admittedly the American was playing under the strain of championship pressure. Even so, Bruen's golf was extraordinary. It was asking too much to expect the Irish boy to repeat the performance in the Walker Cup. Galleries expected him to shoot under 70, but golf is not like that. The sparkle had gone. His game became slightly bogged down. He did well in the 1939 Amateur Championship at Hoylake until he met Alex Kyle. The Scotsman's game was then at its peak. The result was never in doubt. The Open at St Andrews saw Bruen bracketed alongside Henry Cotton as joint favourite. Qualifying rounds confirmed the ranking. Sixty-nine on the Old Course was matched the next day on the New. The total of 138 led the field by 4 shots. Again the sparkle disappeared. He began with 72 and ended with 76 to finish first amateur and equal seventh, an excellent showing for an amateur, yet fell short of what many felt was possible.

It is idle to speculate what might have happened had the war years not intervened. I believe we had in Bruen an amateur capable of winning the Amateur and Open titles on both sides of the Atlantic had he taken the trouble to work at his game. Birkdale, 1946, supplied the answer in part. Two hundred and eighty-six entered for the Amateur Championship, form was in the melting-pot, prewar reputations meant next to nothing. The record book shows that Bruen won by beating Bobby Sweeny 4 and 3. It looks impressive, but I question whether our major amateur honour has ever been won with the assistance of so many recovery shots. No one could claim that Bruen had a graceful style. A purist would damn it outright as ugly. He drove the ball prodigious distances, but excessive length without control can be disastrous, particularly at Birkdale, where the willow scrub breaks the heart of any wayward golfer. In Bruen's case it proved distracting without being fatal. Efforts to extricate himself from unplayable lies resulted in three smashed clubs. One hole in particular in the final was memorable. Playing against a strong wind and torrential rain, Bruen found the 517-yard fourteenth in two glorious shots. Bruen deserved the Amateur title, but it was not won with golf worthy of his skill. The 1951 Walker Cup match, again at Birkdale, saw the Irish player, now burly-framed and man-sized, tackle another Walker Cup examination. Two years earlier at Winged Foot, he had been beaten 5 and 4 by Skee Reigel and 2 and 1 in partnership with Sam McCready against the US pairing of Frank Stranahan and Charles Kocsis. Birkdale revealed yet again a wrist weakness. He finished the foursome virtually a passenger, having to play shots one-handed.

That was the last we saw of Bruen in major championship events. It was sad for this country rarely produces such rich golfing material that falls short of fulfilling its promise. His method of hitting the ball was unique. Few could imitate his style to advantage. The famous 'loop' at the top of the backswing had to be seen to be believed. How the idiosyncracy was ironed out during the downswing was a matter for speculation and high-speed photography to prove. Maybe it proves that it doesn't really matter how you hit the ball provided it is struck firm, square, straight, and far. James Bruen was a law unto himself. If only his youthful enthusiasm had lasted a few more seasons.

17

A Galaxy of Champions

THE Sixties produced several impressive champions, men whose shot-making is still remembered. One of these was Tony Lema, once described as a mini-carboncopy of Walter Hagen. There were certainly similarities. Lema was ambitious, at times extrovert, but in a way self-consciously contrived compared with the spontaneous showmanship of the Haig. Nevertheless, Lema was immensely popular with the crowds. Success had not been easy. His father, a labourer of Portugese extraction, died when he was three, leaving the penniless mother to cope with four young children in the industrial slums of Oakland, California. Tony was a typical boy of that background. Truant from school, anything to earn the odd dollar, including caddying at the municipal course. He worked as a bottle-washer in San Francisco, served two years in the Marines in Korea, then took a job as an assistant golf professional. An uncontrolled temper did not help. Once that was mastered, he made progress, but was still an also-ran. The turning-point came when, after he had failed to qualify for the 1961 American Open, Horton Smith in Detroit ironed out his putting faults. Confidence on the greens produced results. Two years later Lema won his first title in the Orange County Open Championship, after a play-off with Bob Rosburg.

When Lema arrived at St Andrews in 1964 he had won four of the last five tournaments in the United States and was riding the crest of the wave, but had still to gain a major championship. He left it late. There was time for only two practice rounds on the Old Course. Even with Tip Anderson as a caddie, the odds were against him with a field of 327, including such names as Jack Nicklaus, Peter Thomson, Gary Player, Bob Charles, and

Roberto de Vicenzo. The weather did little to help. Gale-force winds left half the entry with scores in the 80s. Peter Thomson and Bob Charles had 79. Nicklaus drove the last green with the wind behind in a round of 76. Christy O'Connor and Jean Garaialde shared the lead on 71. Lema returned 73. The second day was calmer. Nicklaus had a round of 74 which included 40 putts. Lema played superbly for a four under par 68 which put him in the lead by two shots. On the last day Nicklaus looked out of the chase, trailing Lema by nine strokes, but he struck a purple patch, highlighted on the twelfth where he sank a 60-foot putt for 3 to be five under par. Tension had caught up with Lema. His nine-shot lead had shrunk to two. Nicklaus went into lunch with a six under par 66.

In the final round it was Nicklaus who faltered at the fourth and fifth, but rallied strongly with 3-4-2-3 to be out in 34. Lema responded with 4-3-3-3-4-3 to equal the 34. Nicklaus added another 34 for the inward half. His aggregate of 284 meant that on the tenth tee Lema had a seven-shot lead. Apart from hiccups at the twelfth, fourteenth and seventeenth, Lema was in a safe position at the home hole. Only a disaster could snatch the title. A useful drive left him eighty yards short with the Valley of Sin to clear. Lema played an old-fashioned Scottish invented run-up to four feet short of the pin, sank the putt for a birdie and became Open Champion by a margin of five strokes, a win worthy of a true champion. Tragically, Tony and his wife died in an air crash on the way to a tournament in America. He is remembered as an amiable young man with a graceful swing and determination to reach the top. He once said that he found it astonishing that a golfer so highly strung as Gary Player should win a major championship. He met the South African in the final of the World Match-Play Championship. Standing 7 up with 17 to play, it looked as if Player had confirmed Lema's remarks. He overlooked the fact that highly strung golfers can be tenacious. The South African achieved one of his finest victories.

Another outstanding winner of the Open was Bob Charles, who made it at Lytham in 1963 after a play-off with Phil Rodgers. Left-handed golfers, many of whom feel that the odds are stacked against them, received a tonic when the New Zealander won the title. They maintain that the topography of courses is unfavourable for them, the argument being that the lay-outs are meant for the right-handed player. There is an element of truth in the assertion. Golf architects are usually right-handed and the average course is designed with this class of player in mind. The counter argument is that a well-hit shot gets its true reward. The siting of traps,

The death of Tony Lema and his wife in an air crash on the way to a tournament was a great loss. His victory in the Open by 5 shots from Jack Nicklaus was immensely popular.

Bob Charles's victory in the Open at Lytham was a tonic for left-handed golfers who argue that the topography of courses benefit right-handed players. In the case of Charles, he seems to have better controlled clubhead speed than his right-handed opponents. He is the southpaw supreme.

however, usually shows that a poor tee-shot finds a bunker intended to penalize a slice. The design of greens should be equally fair to a carefully placed shot, whether to right or left.

Some professionals argue that good left-handed golf is rare. That argument presupposes that man is instinctively right-handed. It is suggested that a child with a natural left-handed tendency should be trained to use the right hand. The danger is that for some people the left hand is their master hand and to change to the right would put them at a disadvantage. They are neither left-handed nor right-handed. There have been instances when naturally left-handed people, like Walter Hagen and Bobby Jones, played golf right-handed, which proves that being ambidextrous does not mean mediocre results.

Bob Charles silenced critics by the quality of his shot-making. His style remained convincing over a long period. Comparing him to his right-handed opponents, he seemed to have better controlled clubhead speed. Not particularly powerful in build, he compensated with exceptionally strong hands, wrists and forearms. His grip was most impressive. It might have been moulded to the shaft. Throughout the swing the grip was firm. The way his hands took the clubhead through the ball was an object lesson on how the speed of the swing can be regulated. His putting style was convincing. There was never a hint of tension or over-tightening of the forearm muscles. The New Zealander was an incomparable holer-out. He is remembered as the southpaw supreme.

Tony Jacklin set the golf world alight when in less than a year he achieved the double of winning the Open Championships of this country and America, to be followed by a bleak period when only flashes of this form were shown and major honours proved elusive. He was in the wilderness for so long that some observers felt he might retire from championship events in favour of a lucrative club appointment. Happily he stayed on the circuit. Something of the old flair returned, maybe not in actually competing but by demonstrating a remarkable flair for leadership. His enthusiasm and tactical skills were largely responsible for inspiring Ryder Cup victories over America, not only in this country but on their soil. Jacklin was a crowd-puller. Few professionals on the European circuit commanded such respect. He was the complete golfer.

Gary Player's record is one long catalogue of success. It includes three Open titles; Muirfield 1959, Carnoustie 1968, and Lytham 1974; the American Open 1965; two American PGA titles, 1962 and 1972; three wins in the Masters; and continued successes on the Veterans' circuit. He

Tony Jacklin set the golf world alight when in less than a year he won the Open Championship and the US Open. Since then he has inspired by his brilliant captaincy of the victorious British Ryder Cup team.

is only the third player to win the four major competitive events. Another peak remains. He wanted to achieve the feat of winning a major title in four decades, from the 1950s to the 1980s. Unfortunately time ran out, but even now he has the skill, experience and determination to be in contention in any championship. His style is distinctive with occasional idiosyncrasies that suggest a miracle might be necessary, but the result is usually on target. If a golfer swings off his feet at the completion of a drive, anything is possible. In Player's case, the ball invariably sailed down the fairway. Under pressure he reacts with pin-point accuracy. Match-play brings out an aggressive streak that refuses to acknowledge defeat as shown in his epic World Match-Play Championship final against Tony Lema when he clawed his way back to victory.

I group together Arnold Palmer, Tom Watson and Jack Nicklaus, three giants who between them conquered the world of golf. Through the medium of televison their skills become known to millions. Close-up shots by the cameras froze tense moments when victories were gained under terrific pressures. No other golfer reflects so truly the tremendous con-centration needed in the closing stages of a championship as Nicklaus. The sense of awareness almost freezes on the screen. Palmer applies just as much mental application but his style is freer, more flowing, like his swing. Watson has a perpetual youthfulness that never ages. His reflexes are more predictable and he registers anxiety and disappointment by comparison with more poker-faced opponents. This trio have been supreme examples of how golf should be played when the stakes are great. In defeat their sportsmanship has always been manifest and victory was accepted without undue display of feelings. In many ways they were too good to be true. Each one exercised immense influence on the game. They are an integral part of the history of golf.

The Seventies produced a rich quota of outstanding performances, many by golfers who have ensured their niche in history, occasionally not by success but through tragic errors. One such was Doug Sanders, the thirty-seven-year-old professional from Georgia, who was not seriously con-sidered as a contender for the 1970 Open and had to compete in the qualifying rounds at Panmure. In the actual championship wind and rain swept across St Andrews, decimating the field. Trevino coped best. After the third round he was two shots better than Nicklaus, Jacklin and Sanders. Conditions worsened for the final round. Chances were blown away. It became a straight duel between Nicklaus and Sanders, the issue turning on the last two holes. Nicklaus settled for par at the Road Hole. Sanders skirted disaster. His second was bunkered, recovered brilliantly to a couple of feet from the hole and saved par. At the home hole Nicklaus was overstrong. An uphill putt from the Valley of Sin finished twenty feet past the hole. Sanders had a useful drive, overstrong second, leaving two putts to win. The first finished a foot from the hole. The title was there to be claimed. After what seemed an eternity whilst nerves were steadied, Sanders played and missed. The title had gone. The play-off was close, 72 to 73, but for Doug Sanders it was a cruel experience. One incident can affect a player's career, and an unlucky break can make the difference between fame and obscurity. Those of us who watched will remember the agony of the moment. It should have been a mere formality. Nicklaus had been ready to offer congratulations. It was unbelievable, then to lose the play-off by one shot. Happily there was no danger of Sanders disappearing into limbo. He was a seasoned campaigner, but undoubtedly that muffed putt affected his career and balance.

It is interesting to speculate how golfing history might have been altered had a putt not been missed. The 'if only' of golf can be ironic.

Jack Newton almost became Open Champion at Carnoustie in 1975. He tied with Tom Watson on 279, only to finish one stroke behind in the play-off. The Australian virtually had the trophy in his hands, but putts missed by inches killed the hope. Peter Oosterhuis had his chances in 1974, but they slipped away and Gary Player triumphed. The tall Englishman later enjoyed a measure of success, but many failures. Had he won the 1974 Championship, the psychological boost might have started a winning streak. Sometimes it has the opposite effect, as Tony Jacklin discovered. After winning the world's two major Open titles, Jacklin slumped into decline as opportunities slipped away.

Had honours gone to the runners-up, honours would have been scattered much wider. Injustices righted by the addition to the roster of such names as Christy O'Connor, Sen. and Brian Huggett. Both finished two shots behind Peter Thomson at Birkdale in 1965. Either was more than qualified for such recognition. Their hearts were big enough to beat the world's best. In 1978 the Open title could have gone to Tom Kite, Simon Owen, Ray Floyd or Ben Crenshaw. The last named saw his chances snatched away again in 1979. Jack Nicklaus could have gained the title on no less than seven occasions if the runner-up slot counted. Bob Charles could have won in 1968 and 1969. In the Fifties, that outstanding Belgian professional, Flory van Donck would twice have been Open Champion, a feat that might have been equalled by Johnny Bulla, Antonio Cerda, James Adams and Frank Stranahan.

A golfer who should have been Open Champion was Dai Rees. This half-pint-sized Welshman came so near, but every time a jinx upset the final round. When the Open was resumed after the Second World War, he was bracketed in the lead after three rounds with Sam Snead and Johnny Bulla. The first hole on the Old Course, St Andrews, is straightforward. Rees needed eight shots, a millstone that left him 5 strokes behind the winner. On the runner-up roll, Rees could have been Champion three times. Other worthy additions would have been Phil Rodgers, Dave Thomas twice, Johnny Fallon, a quiet methodical player who epitomized consistency, Neil Coles, unflappable and unobtrusive, and Leo Diegel with his unusual putting style. Memories fade, but the records help us to remember such men as Macdonald Smith. Suave and cool, he was in a class of his own, one of the finest players who never won the championship. He could have been Open Champion twice. Other first-timers would have included the massive Archie Compston, legendary Fred Robson, inimitable Harry Bradshaw, aggressive Craig Wood, orthodox Syd Scott, gritty Reg Horne. An unexpected name would have been Liang Huan Lu, the courteous runner-up to Lee Trevino at Birkdale in 1971.

Such a rota proves that in championships, only the winner counts. To be runner-up is gratifying, but the feat is only remembered as long as the presentation ceremony lasts. 'Also-rans' sadly do not make history.

Johnny Miller was another who knew the heights, only to languish afterwards. So marked was his decline that he slumped to 111th place in the American rankings with winnings of $17,440 compared with his peak seasons with victories in seventeen US tournaments, including the 1973 American Open followed by the 1976 Open at Birkdale. Stake money for such success came to $353,021. Then, as with Jacklin, the urge to win came back and once again Miller's name featured on the marker-boards. Dissimilar in appearance, both players were enormous favourites with galleries on both sides of the Atlantic.

Lee Trevino was one of the most successful professionals on the US tour. He had to contend with a back injury that affected his swing but not his winning streak. Since he won the American Open in 1968, his tally of success was remarkably consistent. Five major championships and twenty-six international tournaments stood to his credit, plus five World Cup and five Ryder Cup appearances. Volatile, wisecracking and unpredictable, the Mexican concealed feelings and intention with entertaining repartee.

Behind the clowning was a calculating professional who followed a clear-cut shot routine. He is not a slasher. Few players have such control over their strategy, particularly his use of the fade. His style is uncomplicated, quick decision-making, little delay in playing shots with pronounced wrist-action, and, at times, a sensitive and effective putter.

Entirely different was David Graham, a golfer who cannot be judged by first impressions. These are invariably unflattering unless you like a tight-lipped, supercilious veneer. The Australian seems to like this image, yet beneath the dour exterior is a friendly, almost sensitive individual. He has had a hard life from childhood and when every simple privilege has to be earned, the tough part of such a struggle inevitably leaves its mark. It had to be an aloof, almost lonely, personal fight to make the grade. It began when, as a lad of fourteen, he took his first job in the professional's shop. After an abortive spell as a club professional, he began work in a golf club factory.

Graham's love of golf has persisted from childhood when he won the Tasmanian junior championship. At that time he was a left-hander, switching to the right hand when he became a professional. As his golfing career took shape so he seemed to develop the rough, abrasive exterior, the disdainful air touched with a note of resentment. The best thing that happened to him was when he married in Australia at the age of twenty-one. He and Maureen moved to Dallas and he became so immersed in the American way of life that it is surprising he has not sought American citizenship. In a way Graham moulded himself on the austere likeness of Ben Hogan. They have many features in common. When Ben is with his wife Valerie, he becomes a warm, outgoing individual. The same applies to Graham when he is with Maureen. Underneath the hard surface are really nice people. The trouble is that only a few are privileged to see that side.

The tall, cheerful figure of Tom Weiskopf, with his distinctive stride and mannerisms, quickly caught the public imagination when he won the Open Championship at Troon. His form was unpredictable. At times his shot-making is superb, then, without warning, he could play strokes that gave encouragement to long-handicap spectators. The classic instance was in the 1980 Masters. At the 155-yard twelfth, he misjudged the tee-shot. The ball hit the bank and went into the creek. The second ball suffered the same fate. The third ball reached the green but rolled back into the water. The fourth also found the creek. The fifth finished short but likewise ended in the water. The sixth effort stayed on the green but two putts from seven yards meant 13 on the card. And in the next round he put two more tee-shots into the water and carded an average of ten for one hole. These were extreme examples, but the fact remains that Tom Weiskopf is good value from the spectators' point of view, though not necessarily from the historian's.

Tom Watson was continually in the news during the Seventies. He triumphed in anonymous fashion. He lacked the flamboyant approach of Trevino. He could not match the physical attributes of Nicklaus. There was no sign of the intense concentration of Player. He was not a loner, yet no one could say that Watson was extrovert. He strode the fairways mentally aloof. His self-analytical mind could almost be heard working. In that sense, Tom Watson was a fellow apart. His natural boyish grin endeared him to galleries and viewers like an ageless Cheshire Cat. He had and still has the image of the college boy who has made good. Perhaps the finest tribute that can be paid to him is the fondness that people behind the scenes had for him. And this was acquired without any facility on his part, for his personality does not project in forms of extroverted bonhomie. It is simply that everyone who knows him acquires such respect for his seriousness of purpose, that, through no conscious effort on his part, he became surrounded by admirers. Tom Watson has become a golfing possession.

In the seasons that were a run-up to the Nineties, several golfers came to the forefront, the majority with spasmodic bursts of brilliance that could not be sustained. The skills were there, but fell short of history-making feats. Bill Rogers, the 1981 Open champion, comes in this category. When he came to Wentworth for the 1979 Suntory World Matchplay Championship he was virtually unknown in this country: before that he had been placed 29th on the 1977 American tour and 17th the following year when he won the Bob Hope Desert Classic. At Wentworth he made immediate impact by beating the US Open champion Hale Irwin, and the Augusta Masters winner, Fuzzy Zeller, before defeating Isao Aoki in the final by one hole. His popularity rating with spectators was instantaneous. In 1981 he narrowly failed to win the US Open at Merion; then, partly due to the persuasion of Crenshaw, the Texan entered for the Open. He did not echo Tom Watson's criticism but stated before the competition began that it was one of the finest tests he had tackled. It was unpredictable and demanding. Placing drives was of paramount importance. It paid dividends in his case because Rogers could not be classed as one of the longest drivers. His nerve stood the test, particularly on the last afternoon when the lead shrank to one stroke. It might have all collapsed. Instead he came back in style to win the title. He could so easily have joined Trevino and Hogan who won the British Open and US Open in the same year. From start to finish Rogers never put a foot wrong. The sequel was not so happy. He has never recaptured that spontaneous form. The magic evaporated.

Tom Kite is another American who skirts success when he should be winning. This little man with huge glasses and distinctive style has col- lected cheques at most events, but the winner's cheque always went to someone else. Sympathy is muted by the fact that Kite in spite of losing out on national titles has nevertheless topped the million-dollar mark. Nothing could be more removed from the image created by men like Nicklaus and Watson than that unpredictable professional Craig Stadler, whose talent finally became recognized when he won the Masters at Augusta. There is no one quite like this comfortably built Californian with a rolling gait. He is 5 feet 10 inches tall, weighs over 16 stones, looks unathletic, has a belly suggestive of a bars-darts player contained in a pullover too small, luxuriant moustache that droops, and a reputation for throwing a tantrum. Admittedly he has an unbuttoned look, but appearances can be deceptive. Behind that sloppy exterior is an incisive, technical shot-maker. When the chips are down his game is as ruthless as Nicklaus'. There is no better model for golfers similarly built on a massive scale. He is down-to-earth with all our physical problems. His memory may be limited, but in the meantime ordinary golfers, out of condition and overweight, should note the modifications to his swing enforced by a substantial waistline and be thankful that so much flesh can beat the lean, kempt youngsters.

Another professional who promised much but failed to deliver was Brian Barnes. Something of an extrovert, he attacked the ball in flamboyant fashion. In the early days he hit first and thought afterwards, often in the rough. Temperamentally impulsive and eager for action, Barnes took time to calm down. He once referred to the po-faced kids who appeared in Europe and America as rookies, a conveyor-belt system that churned out moulds all looking the same, without a smile or apparent sense of humour. Why should the public pay good money to watch such anonymous mer- chants. In such company Barnes stood out like a breath of fresh air. He lightened many a dull day with his popular image of pipe-smoking, foaming tankard heavyweight, hat festooned with fish-hooks, periodically striding across the fairways in abbreviated, too tight shorts and dark glasses. He had that magnetic quality known as charisma and once collected the award as White Horse Whisky's personality of the year. Maybe that will be his passport to posterity.

Entirely different is Mark James. He is unpredictable. In team events he shines, and could reach the heights if only temperament was under control. Not always noted for tact and diplomacy, he tends to go round like a lonely, withdrawn and at times disconsolate man. When things go wrong, he slumps, shoulders droop, he visibly wilts. There is no need for an opponent to fight, James beats himself. Successful golfers like Palmer, Trevino and Miller do not slouch around as if suicide-bent. Yet, in relaxed mood, James is pleasant and agreeable. No one likes a sulk, certainly not golfing galleries, and the stupid part is that the real Mark James is as likeable as any of his colleagues. If only he could unbend and relax, even give a genuine smile or make a pleasantry, the public response would be immediate.

Severiano Ballesteros was the best thing that happened to golf for many years. The competitive days of Arnold Palmer had become limited, Gary Player was approaching the veteran stage. It was impossible to predict the future of a rejuvenated Jack Nicklaus, but even he, sooner or later, would be on the sidelines. There was Tom Watson, brilliant but pleasantly anonymous. Ballesteros arrived on the scene in D'Artagnan-style. He produced a cavalier approach not seen since the days of Walter Hagen, competing with an assurance that belied the fact he was only a youngster. He came to the forefront in the 1976 Open at Birkdale when, with the aid of outrageous recoveries, he finished equal second with Nicklaus behind the winner, Johnny Miller. And this was from an inexperienced lad who was born in Santander on 9 April 1957. Since then he has gone from strength to strength, collecting international titles, large cheques, with possibly the realization that he had won the Augusta Masters in 1980 giving immense satisfaction. He had become only the second non-American to win the title in the forty-four-year history of this prestigious event, Gary Player being the first in 1961. One weakness has been his Latin temperament which quickly becomes depressed. Disappointments and setbacks tend to have a lingering effect. With maturity that reaction is more under control. His natural talent requires free expression. At the outset his swashbuckling style paid dividends by sheer impetuosity. He introduced a new, exciting element into the game. That magic is no longer spontaneous. The 1990 season saw him struggling to regain the old form. It was not kind to his reputation, but such is the Spaniard's talent and

Severiano Ballesteros has demonstrated how a cavalier style of play and a boldness of method can dominate opponents and courses alike. He is a flamboyant shot-maker, reminiscent of Walter Hagen with a d'Artagnan touch. He has stamped his personality on the professional scene in Europe and America.

confidence the setback can only be temporary. The future is still rich with possibilities.

Platinum-haired Greg Norman is a curious mixture of extremes. Nothing appears to perturb him. His face has the anonymity of granite. He has a dry, almost acrid Australian sense of humour, sometimes funnier than he realizes. Being a reasonably immodest kind of fellow, Norman sees himself status-wise on a par with the likes of Nicklaus, Hogan, Watson and Snead, all legends in their lifetime. So do many others, of course, but the Australian is no Walter Mitty. Norman has more panache than most of his colleagues and can take setbacks without behaving like a martyr. One ambition has been to beat another Australian's record in the Open, Peter Thomson's four wins in five years. The feat is not impossible with his impeccable power game, but time is running out.

Bernhard Langer is the first German to claim international ranking. It was not an easy passage. His father was a bricklayer in Augsburg. The only way to golf was as a caddie. He began as a boy, became professional at fifteen, and won the German National Championship two years later from a field of 150. Jan Brugelmann, a Cologne industrialist, recognized Langer's potential and became his sponsor. Results on both sides of the Atlantic have confirmed such faith. Langer has made the grade in spite of an attack of putting 'yips' that undermined his confidence. Constant practice and an occasional gimmick have helped to ease this putting hesitancy that seems to attack successful players. Outwardly Langer possesses the ice-cold isolation shown some years ago by Bjorn Borg, with similar physique, broad chest, strong forearms and the sturdy legs of a skier. When Langer returns home to the small Bavarian town of Diedorf, he must know that he has the skill to beat the world's best.

The same can be said about Sandy Lyle. There have been enough purple patches to show that he ranks among the world's best. Nothing he does is strained or arid. His technical equipment is sound. On the links, in his own vein and given the breaks, he has few superiors. In a Scottish way he is aware that he possesses star quality, yet at times confidence becomes undermined. 1990 was a nightmare season. Nothing went right. His form was erratic. Success will return. Failure to beat the cut will be cured by sheer determination. At one stage in his career, Lyle had an unusual way to prepare for important events. For some reason best known to himself, he left inadequate time to get acclimatized. A minimum of practice, poor planning, and it-will-be-OK-on-the-day attitude did nothing to help. For instance, when he tried to qualify for the Inverrary Classic in Florida, he went out with a brand new set of clubs that only arrived the day before he left. Hardly sensible timing. In the US Open at Merion, he only allowed himself two rounds of practice over this difficult course in temperatures of 95 degrees and humidity about 90 per cent. With such scanty course preparation and climate acclimatization, only a purblind optimist could expect to do well. Lyle learnt the hard way. The chore of getting to know a course was systematically followed by the likes of Watson and Nicklaus. In spite of their vast experience, they went through the routine. Lyle took note that if they felt the need for such painstaking preparation, it might be a good idea to follow their example. The routine paid rich dividends.

America continues to turn out highly skilled professionals like Curtis Strange, Payne Stewart, Paul Azinger, Mark Calcavecchia, Fred Couples and Larry Mize; Europe has Ian Woosnam, Jose-Marie Olazabal and Ronan Rafferty. Each professional could develop into world beaters, but the tendency is to register spasmodic victories. Consistency must be constant if the highest peaks are to be scaled. Nick Faldo is on the threshold of joining the game's illustrious giants. Each made history, but in so doing they retained the values associated with the game. Faldo is fortunate in that he can plan ahead without financial worries. Apart from winnings, like the £85,000 prize money after winning the 1990 Open, lucrative endorsements plus course design projects in Japan were estimated to top the £10-million mark. Be that as it may. The total removes distractions. Nick Faldo still has a long way to go before achieving golfing immortality in spite of the plaudits from some writers too young to know what has gone before. On the evidence of what has been accomplished, there is every likelihood that his ambition will be realized.

18

The Canvas of Women's Golf

NOT MANY people know when women's golf was introduced into these islands. The St Andrews Ladies Club came into existence in 1867 and became so popular that membership soared to 500 in nineteen years. Musselburgh Ladies and London Scottish Ladies were bracketed together in 1872. The latter did not last long but was revived as Wimbledon Ladies in 1890. The first authentic reference to women's golf appears in a minute of the Royal Musselburgh Golf Club dated 14 December 1810. There are two versions of this particular record but the one most commonly quoted reads:

> The Club to present by subscription a handsome new Creel and Shawl to the best Female Golfer, who plays on the annual occasion on the 1st of January next, old style (12th January new), to be intimated to the Fish Ladies by William Robertson, the Officer of the Club.
>
> Two of the best Barcelona Silk Handkerchiefs to be added to the above premium of the Creel.
>
> Alex G. Hunter, Captain

The inference is that the early women golfers were fishing girls, possibly with limited skill but with keen rivalry to win the shawl that was worn afterwards in Musselburgh High Street. There is a slight doubt whether *shawl* is the correct word. It appears in Clark's version but the original refers to a *skull*, which was a type of fish basket.

Some historians suggest that Mary Queen of Scots played golf at St Andrews during her first eighteen-day tour of Scotland after landing from

France and one fanciful researcher has produced a very free translation, or rather paraphrase, of a passage in the sixth book of the *Odyssey* suggesting that Nausicaa, daughter of Alcinous, King of Phaeacia, was a keen golfer. The passage reads: '... Nausicaa with the wrists of ivory, the *liking stroke* struck,' and 'the Queen, now, *for the upstroke*, struck the ball quite wide of the other maids.' We are asked to believe that the first is a delicate approach, while the second visualizes the untam'd Nausicaa playing a tee-shot. A vivid imagination makes anything possible.

One thing is certain. 1893 was an important year for women's golf. It marked the inauguration of the Ladies' Golf Union. The idea came from the Wimbledon Club. Circulars were sent out inviting club representatives to attend a meeting in London on 19 April 1893. Those who accepted were a mixed bag: Great Harrowden Hill, St Andrews, Barnes, Eastbourne, Blackheath, Southdown and Brighton, Holywood, Minchinhampton, Ashdown Forest, Wimbledon, and Lytham St Anne's. A Union was formed after Laidlaw Purves, chairman of the meeting, outlined the value of such an institution.

The same year produced the first Women's Championship, which attracted an entry of thirty-eight. The course was nine holes, the total length for the double round being 4,264 yards. Hazards were unknown, the only suspicion of a trap being at the first and last holes, where a 'cop' flanked by sand had to be carried with the drive. The championship was received with mixed views. Someone said that though the women did not seem to find it difficult to behave like men, nevertheless they found it extremely hard to behave like gentlemen. The standard of play was indifferent, some of their efforts to strike the ball attaining almost the dignity of manual labour, hardly surprising considering the handicap imposed by their clothes. Almost all wore sailor hats precariously perched on top of their heads and held in position by hat-pins, sleeves were exceptionally wide and skirts voluminous.

One eye-witness commented that several women were not so much dressed as upholstered. The exception was the winner, Lady Margaret Scott, daughter of the third Earl of Eldon and member of a family rich in golfing experience. In skill she was superior to anyone else in the field, winning the inaugural event by beating Issette Pearson, who was largely responsible for the LGU system of universal handicapping. Lady Margaret went on to win the title in successive seasons at Littlestone and Portrush, then retired.

Women had not only to contend with clothes that were impracticable when it came to swinging a club but also with popular sentiment like that voiced by Lord Moncrieff as to whether women should be allowed to play golf at all. He suggested that seventy or eighty yards should be the average limit of a drive, then went on to say: 'Not because we doubt a lady's power to make a longer drive but because that cannot well be done without raising the club above the shoulder. Now, we do not presume to dictate, but we must observe that the posture and gestures requisite for a full swing are not particularly graceful when a player is clad in female dress.' He welcomed the advent of women's links on the understanding that they were laid out on a smaller scale than the longer round, he even had no objection to women playing on the 'long course' at set times when male golfers were feeding or resting, but 'at other times they are in the way.' The noble lord did not mince words. He went on, 'We do not know that a claim of absolute equality has yet been made: but the ladies are advancing in all pursuits with such strides, or leaps and bounds, whichever expression may be thought the more respectful, that it will, no doubt, not be long before such a claim is formulated. How is it to be met?' He rejected the suggestion that ladies might play with men over the longer round by referring to observations made by a young player who 'found it hard to decide between flirtation and playing the game, declaring "It's all mighty pleasant, but it's not business."'

Patronizing, sexist remarks were frequent at that time. It was not long before men retreated in silence. Snide comments were silenced by the remarkable way in which women became proficient at the game. It reached the point when Glenna Collett Vare ventured the prophecy: 'The idea of a woman winning the Open Championship in competition with the sterner, longer-driving sex is not so fantastic as it would seem.' No one took the words seriously. The idea was too silly to be considered. Shortly afterwards the suggestion did not look so ridiculous. No one was predicting that a female could win the Open from the stronger sex, but the standard of shot-making had so improved with a small group of women golfers that they would probably show a clean pair of heels to quite a section of the male entry in open competitions. I think of Mildred 'Babe' Zaharias. This American entered for the British Ladies' Championship and crushed all opposition in sensational fashion. Against some opponents she outdrove them to the tune of one hundred yards. Success led to an offer to turn professional. This she did. Subsequent matches with top-flight American professionals, to say nothing of the devastating treatment meted out to prominent male amateurs who tried in vain to beat her, increased respect

Mildred 'Babe' Zaharias who stood out as the most powerful shot-maker in women's golf. Her prediction that a woman golfer could finish in the top ten in the Open Championship has not been realized. Had sexism not proved too influential, Mildred in her prime would have cut many professionals down to size.

for her reputation. Louise Suggs and Patsy Berg likewise changed their amateur status with similar success. Had these golfers entered for the American or Open Championships, the odds are that many men would have returned higher cards.

To the present generation Zaharias is a mythical figure. Her playing career was short for she died of cancer at the age of forty-two in the autumn of 1956. Even so she was the outstanding woman golfer of the day. Free from inhibitions, she was a phenomenal attraction, the first American to win the British Women's title. Before she turned to golf, Mildred Didrickson had broken world records in the 1932 Olympic Games at Los Angeles, winning gold medals for the hurdles and javelin and broke the record for the high jump by several inches. She came of Scandinavian stock. Her parents were Norwegian and came from Oslo, and emigrated to Port Arthur in the Gulf of Mexico. By the time they moved to Beaumone there were seven young Didricksons, five girls and two boys. On leaving school, Mildred worked for an insurance company in Dallas living in a room at five dollars a month.

Her debut as a golfer was on a driving-range in Dallas. The first drive was over 250 yards. That was to be her attitude to the game. To see her competing against other women was like watching Jack Nicklaus playing in a boy's championship. Opponents were outdriven by fully a hundred yards. Her shots had the incisiveness and power of a professional. There was nothing pretty or dainty about her style. The ball was there to be hit. And hit it she did with every ounce of strength. Few women have had such a powerful back or such strong leg muscles which belied her slender, graceful build and highly developed dress sense. Mildred was both feminine and feline. Her nickname 'Babe' was derived from the famous Babe Ruth, the baseball player.

Completely extrovert, Mildred revelled in describing how she played and beat without the aid of strokes every member of the American men's Walker Cup team. During a round over the punishing championship links of Muirfield she had not wanted anything in excess of an 8 iron for her second shots. I always regretted that the British Professional Golfers' Association declined to accept her entry for the Open Championship. Had she competed there was every chance of finishing in the first ten, which would have left quite a number of professionals with red faces.

On the last day of the British Ladies' Championship at Gullane, I saw her arrive in red-and-white check gingham shorts. Old prejudices never seem to be forgotten. The lady captain of Gullane persuaded the American to return to the hotel and swap the offending garment for conventional blue corduroy slacks. She did so with good grace, then surprised the officials by vaulting over a six-foot railing in front of the first tee. After the Gullane success, Mildred again turned professional and began a barn-storming tour of the States. In the process she accumulated a bevy of feminine talent, women golfers who had made their name as amateurs and decided that dollars were more useful than silver plate. She visited England with the circus known as Fred Corcoran's young ladies. The golf she produced would have beaten half the field in any men's tournament. The 'Babe', more than anyone else, put women's golf on the professional map by creating a vital public image matched by a rare skill.

The image of women in sport is all-important. Show-jumping and lawn tennis are obvious examples where appearances and performance match. Golf should be in the same category, only unfortunately the public image of women golfers is poor. They only have themselves to blame because they refuse to co-operate. Today the curtain-raiser to the women's golf season is the Avia Watches International Foursomes at The Berkshire, and often played in conditions more suitable for winter sports. One of the organizers, Joan Rothschild, disappointed by the entrants' appearance, recently offered a special prize for the best-dressed player. Her comments were apt:

I am frequently dismayed by the way golfers are turned out. Men dress badly, but women are even worse. Very few seem to bother how they look on the course. They turn up in old jeans or a crushed and tatty skirt that they keep only for golf. It is not good enough and doesn't happen in other sports. It does not cost a lot to dress nicely and if you are well turned out, it can boost your ego and help you play better.

The following year Joan Rothschild went one better. She complained bitterly that the golfers still shambled round in shapeless clothes. There was no need to appear on the links 'looking like a sack of potatoes'. The judge awarded one entrant, who shall be nameless, half-a-point out of ten – and that was charity. A statistical survey revealed that only a quarter of the entry of over 300 required larger sizes. Most measured 37-26-37 which meant that theoretically they were in good shape, though at times it was difficult to believe.

For some reason this trait is common. Women, well-groomed and smart at home and on social occasions, walk the fairways like dowdy creatures, an appearance for many years seemingly condoned, if not encouraged, by the Ladies' Golf Union, whose attitude has been puritanical. Extremes in garb or mannerisms were bad taste. Players who attempted to create a popular personality image were frowned upon. If official advice was ignored at LGU events, trouble followed. This happened in a big way at Westward Ho during the 1933 English Championship. Gloria Minoprio shattered LGU equanimity by stepping up to the first tee in immaculately-cut black slacks, close-fitting black tunic up to the neck, black toque and dead-white complexion caused by protective cream to prevent sunburn. From head to foot this tall, slender girl was in jet black. Had she appeared in the nude, officials could not have been more affected. Officials and competitors met in the clubhouse and formally expressed regret at the first appearance of slacks in a championship and deplored the departure from normal dress. Additional consternation was caused through Gloria using only one club, a cleek which was adapted for all emergencies. A caddie followed behind carrying a spare in case it broke. This was the first time a woman golfer had hit the headlines because of what she wore. It was also a classic example of psychological gamesmanship – opponents panicked at the thought of their full armoury of clubs being beaten by a lone club.

When the English Championship was played at Hayling Island, I refereed the Minoprio match against a Miss James, a far superior shot-maker who played like a mesmerized rabbit and was beaten. Afterwards in the clubhouse a wager with Henry Longhurst was settled. In the clubhouse Gloria never sat down. I maintained that was because her slacks were so tight and narrow it would have been hazardous, if not impossible. I was right in part. Tight straps under the shoes ensured that her trousers were without creases, but the strain of sitting might have been too much.

The 1948 Curtis Cup match between Great Britain and the United States of America at Birkdale provided another example of LGU convention. For the duration of the event the clubhouse was taken over by the women. Before lunch on the first day I rushed into the changing-room to find that not only had it been commandeered but the stalls had been hidden by draped flags to avoid embarrassing the females. It became necessary to lower the Union Jack to half-mast before nature could have its way. Today all that has changed with America taking the lead. Women's professional golf across the Atlantic is now big business. Players are sponsored and marketed like commercial commodities. Stake-money is substantial, provided the projected image is spot-on with current trends. In this field British women professionals got off to a slow start. At the outset few of them could attract a gallery. Shot-making ability was lacking, charisma an unknown word. Rounds of 80 and 85, even 90s could hardly inspire spectators, whilst appearances tended to match the scores. Happily the situation is much better, skills are more evident, whilst prize money has substantially increased. It has sunk home that strong, colourful characters are necessary before a shot is struck. In short, someone like Mildred 'Babe' Zaharias, one of the most remarkable sporting females America has produced. Completely extrovert, at times she made a point of upsetting old-fashioned etiquette, like the occasion when a Ladies Golf Union official congratulated her on marrying a gentleman who was an eminent all-in wrestler. The good wishes were acknowledged, plus the loud aside . . . 'and it took him a fortnight to throw me!' It also required an interval before the remark was explained. In more ways than one Mildred was a significant influence in revolutionizing women's golf.

Equally effective in a more unassuming way was one of the most versatile of nineteenth-century sportswomen, Lottie Dod. She made her golfing debut at Littlestone in 1894; was Lawn Tennis Champion no fewer than five times, first at the age of sixteen in 1887, 1888, 1891, 1892 and 1893, after which she retired unbeaten; won the Skating Championship; was an international hockey player; successful member of the Alpine Club; skilful archer; outstanding billiards player; won the Ladies Golf Championship in 1904, and was semi-finalist in 1898 and 1899. In every way Lottie was ahead of her time.

The same could be said of Lady Margaret Scott, later Lady Hamilton Russell, who won the inaugural Open Amateur in 1893 and the following two years, a feat only equalled by Cecil Leitch (1914–20–21) and Enid Wilson (1931–32–33). As was the case with Mildred Zaharias, she out-classed and outdrove all her contemporaries. She went even further, entering a Championship at Cheltenham in 1892 as the only woman in an all-male entry and won decisively. At Bath she returned the best scratch score of 70, a record. Looking through the photographs of all past champions, I would say she ranks as one of the prettiest and most feminine in leg-o'-mutton sleeves with tiny wasp waist. After her third win, she retired from championship golf, maybe because no one could extend her. After her third win her father, Lord Eldon, offered to present the LGU with a replica of the trophy and to retain the original for his daughter. The LGU demurred, retained the cup, whilst the noble lord had a replica made for his daughter.

Other lady pioneers in style and dress whose contributions were sig-

Charlotte (Lottie) Dod won the Open Amateur in 1904, having switched from champion tennis player to golfer. She had won the Ladies Lawn Tennis Championship at Wimbledon at the age of fifteen in 1887 and won it four times after before 1893. Five years later, she showed her golfing prowess by holing the full course on the championship links at Hoylake in 90, the best score then made by a lady. She felt strongly that women do not observe the 'supreme sporting spirit.' To quote her words: 'It has always been a reproach against women that they never care to keep strictly to the rules of whatsoever game it pleases them to play. That may have been so in the past, when ladies were but novices in the pursuit of athletics and had not time to imbibe the true spirit of games, which men had done for generations. Still, it makes it only the more important for us all to strive so to model our behaviour that we may truthfully be called, in more sense than one, the fair sex.' Such are the sentiments of almost a century ago.

nificant included Issette Pearson, the first honorary secretary of the Ladies' Golf Union and an outstanding player of her generation, and Cecil Leitch, who played in her first golf competition in 1908 as a girl of seventeen dressed in a mid-calf-length skirt, long-sleeved blouse, spats and hair in a plait. It sounds very ordinary, but in those days caused eyebrows to be raised. Her prowess as a player likewise impressed when she beat the former Open Champion, Harold Hilton, in 1910, a feat that did not escape notice by vocal suffragettes. Other leaders in style included the Irish champion, May Hezlet, eminent member of a well-known golfing family, and Enid Wilson, impressive shot-maker and ideal temperament who made a contribution to the development of women's golf.

My next choice is Pamela Barton, whose death during the Second World War was a grievous loss. The present generation know little or nothing about one of our finest lady golfers. Within the space of a few years she gained major golfing honours. I recall her first appearance in the British Ladies' Championship as a youngster of seventeen. Selected for Surrey's second team, her potential was apparent. She did not disappoint and reached the final on her first Championship appearance. Her Scottish opponent, Helen Holm, was too experienced. Although 3 up at the tenth, the Scot wiped out the deficit after lunch, and went on to win 6 and 5.

The next year the championship was held at Newcastle, Co. Down. One moment I recall. Pam had just beaten Doris Park, daughter of a famous Open Champion, and learnt that she had to play her sister Mervyn in the semi-final, just as the Orr sisters clashed in 1897 and the Hezlets, May and Florence, in 1907. The Newcastle final had a similar ending with Wanda Morgan winning 3 and 2. 1939 saw Pam Barton's finest season. The Championship went to Southport and Ainsdale, the entry strengthened by the challenge of the American Curtis Cup team. Her victims included Diana Plumpton, Jessie Firth, Charlotte Glutting, Doris Wilkins and Kathleen Garnham. In the final against Bridget Newell, she gained the lead at the third and never lost it. The winning margin was 7 and 5. I was not present at Canoe Brook, when she achieved the double by winning the American Ladies' Championship in the same season. The memory of that year recalls a delightfully natural golfer, unspoilt and infectiously happy. Many great women golfers have succeeded since that day, but none have made such a lasting impression.

I have left to the last the greatest lady golfer of all time, Joyce Wethered, later Lady Heathcoat Amory. Her record was remarkable, winning the Ladies Open Amateur Championship in 1922, 1924, 1925 and 1929, and

Lady Heathcoat-Amory (Joyce Wethered). Comparisons are dangerous, but it is possible to say that Joyce Wethered was our greatest woman golfer. No other woman has ever hit the ball so straight with such a flawless swing. Iron shots were played with professional crispness. No one could fault her brassie shots, whilst the short game, on and around the greens, was brilliant. Moreover she was equally good at match- or medal-play.

the English title in 1920, 1921, 1922, 1923 and 1924. Add to this list the Surrey Championship in 1921, 1922, 1924, 1929 and 1932. She captained the British team in the inaugural Curtis Cup match in 1932, played against France in 1931, and in the English international in 1921, 1922, 1923, 1924, 1925 and 1929. She completed a triumphant professional tour of America in 1935, regained her amateur status in 1954 and became first President of the ELGA. After her marriage to Heathcoat Amory, she retired from competitive golf apart from the occasional entry for the Worplesdon Foursomes. A few statistics help. During two years of competitive golf in this country she won seventy-one of her seventy-three matches. During her American tour she broke eighteen course records, defeated many masculine champions, and established herself as the world's top women golfer. Her unhurried swing was a lesson in rhythm, and she was the first woman golfer to adopt the Vardon grip. I cannot better the tribute paid by that shrewd observer Enid Wilson ... 'Miss Wethered was fragile in appearance, and there was nothing of the Amazon about her ... she evolved the most economical method to suit her physique and by shutting out everything of an extraneous nature avoided the strain which others found so sapping. Miss Wethered brought power combined with perfection of style and a hitherto unknown degree of accuracy.' There is little doubt that Joyce Wethered was the most accurate woman golfer, and probably the most formidable competitor of all time. Comparisons are invidious. No one can achieve more than absolute supremacy in their own time, but I cannot imagine that any woman ever had greater or more exact control of a golf ball. She was endowed with a great genius for golf. As an individual she had rare modesty, at the same time showing a personality of compelling strength. She had no conceit about her golf – it was unnecessary. Her powers of concentration almost dehumanized the game; it was astonishingly free of complication. The whole process of her achievements may not have been as free from strain as her manner invariably suggested, but she had balance to a remarkable degree, and the priceless quality of detachment.

19

The Dream Tournament

THE build-up for the Masters Tournament at Augusta National, Georgia, is always the same. It stands out as a focal point in the calendar with an appeal different to that of any other event. To receive an invitation to compete at Augusta is the ambition of every golfer. It is unique. For four days the world is shown how a tournament should be organized. The process is evolutionary. Since its inception in 1934 the brief of those behind the scenes has been to improve a well-nigh faultless set-up. In one sense Augusta can be likened to Wimbledon in that both benefit from the lessons of the past. Unlike other events, the stage remains constant. The only scope left is for manicuring and polishing a proven format. When the paraphernalia is cleared away and the fairways again become deserted, there is a whole year in which the Tournament Improvement Committee can carry out modifications after assessment and approval. Experienced, vigilant watchdogs with a championship background are on duty throughout the tournament and precious little escapes their notice.

Another feature is that the course is set amid a profusion of floral extravagance with purple, white and pink azaleas, yellow jasmine, and white and pink dogwood, set against a backcloth of lush foliage. Bobby Jones was quick to recognize the dramatic effect of a lay-out of such loveliness, but his ambition was not to highlight natural beauty but inaugurate a tournament that in time would mirror everything that was good about the game. He succeeded. The highest standards were set and have been maintained. Since his death the upsurge in commercialism has infiltrated every branch of professional golf, but Augusta has remained aloof. It is significant that stake-money takes a back seat. Elsewhere the press and sponsors emphasize the dollar-bait, the jackpots of the circus. The public is informed that so-and-so has collected thousands of dollars in prize money, and that every time a certain player strikes a ball the cash-till rings. The Order of Merit Table indicates the skill of a player by the amount of cash he has won, and national teams are virtually selected by accountants. The world is informed that so many professionals are dollar-millionaires and therefore better performers than their predecessors who competed for peanuts.

Augusta turns back the clock. The honour of competing is all-important with the coveted Green Jacket as the symbol of victory. By current standards such an attitude is frivolous, but for those who participate it restores a sense of proportion and true values. On the other hand, time does not stand still at Augusta. It is no backwater. Playing, administrative and spectator facilities are beyond rebuke, but the search for even more improvements is continual.

Take the course. Like St Andrews and Hoylake, first impressions are misleading. It looks a straightforward test with few pitfalls or trouble. The rough barely lives up to its name, whilst the bunkers seem anything but vicious. To the purist the lay-out of the Road Hole on the Old Course is sacrosanct. The Railway Sheds have disappeared, but green contours, bunker siting and the road itself are permanent. At Augusta, greens can be redesigned, traps altered, trees removed, even resited, anything is possible under the heading of improvements. There is one safeguard. Alterations are carried out by golf architects who are in sympathy with the Augusta ideals. Water is a significant factor at Augusta, particularly at the eleventh, twelfth, thirteenth, fifteenth and sixteenth. The twelfth is 155 yards long, the shortest hole but exacting, as scorecards testify. Rae's Creek, like a beautified Barry Burn at Carnoustie, guards the front of the green with yawning bunkers at the back. Tom Watson once commented adversely on the frightening speed of the greens. According to the readings of the Stipmeter, the Augusta greens showed a speed of twelve feet against most of those on the tour that read between six and seven: in lay language, a suicidal speed. Green alterations also presented unknown factors. The eleventh had drainage problems so it was reconstructed. A new dam was made across Rae's Creek behind the lake that rims the green. The drainage trouble was solved by laying a network of pipes a foot below the surface through which hot water was pumped. It was felt that this would solve any headache on this particular hole. Whether Tom Wieskopf agreed is a moot point. I doubt if he will ever forget his experience.

The hole is straightforward with little guile. An accurate tee-shot and all should be well. Weiskopf played a relaxed seven iron. The ball hit the bank and rolled into the water. The second ball went straight into the creek. The third ball made the green but rolled back into the water. The fourth dived straight in. The fifth had the same fate after finishing short. The sixth stayed out, but two putts from seven yards finally resulted in 13. A tragedy for this brilliant American golfer, but a crumb of comfort for the army of rabbits who accept such hacking exploits as a way of life.

The Masters is the showpiece of American golf. Past winners include great golfers like Severiano Ballesteros, Bernhard Langer, Sandy Lyle, and Nick Faldo. I mention them first to underline how what was once an American preserve has in recent years been breached by professionals from Europe. To give continuity to the Masters rota, it is appropriate to recall some whose feats have slipped through the sieve of memory, yet who contributed richly to the story of golf. I think of Horton Smith, winner of the inaugural Masters in 1934 and repeating it two years later. He had that intangible quality of weight, as distinct from bulk, by which great players always reveal themselves. His record was impressive. On his twenty-first birthday he won the French Open Championship. Ryder Cup recognition came in 1929, 1933 and 1935. Threatened ill-health interrupted his career. In the fifties he received the Ben Hogan Award for overcoming illness or injury and the Bobby Jones Award for distinguished sportsmanship in golf. Both national awards were fully deserved for Smith left an indelible impression on the golfing scene of his time. He was the man-behind-the-scenes in the creation of the Masters, though credit rightly belongs to the champion of champions, Bobby Jones.

As a golfer Horton Smith was the stylist of the Golden Age with fluent rhythm and delicate touch. A more selfless or generous person it would be hard to find. His talents were many without ever seeming to exhaust his resources. He enjoyed life and the manner of his death at the age of fifty-five was somehow appropriate. In the same way that one of England's soccer legends, 'Dixie' Dean, died during the 1980 Derby match between Liverpool and Everton at Goodison Park, scene of his triumphs and loyalties, so Horton Smith, after attending the Ryder Cup match at Atlanta in 1963, collapsed and died in hospital. Even in the last hours of his life he retained his passionate love for the game.

Other Augusta winners whom time has swallowed up must include Ralph Guldahl, who was an overnight star. This Dallas golfer turned professional in 1932 at the age of twenty. Five years later he won the

United States Open at Oakland Hills with the remarkable aggregate of 281 for seventy-two holes, and repeated the success the following year at Cherry Hills in Denver with a six-stroke margin over Dick Metz. He won the Masters Tournament in 1939. Before that he had won the Western and Augusta Open Championships and was runner-up in the 1937 and 1938 Masters. In 1940 Guldahl was runner-up to Byron Nelson for the National PGA title. Then, from that moment, he went into tournament oblivion. He lost his swing and confidence. To his credit he recognized the fact, retired rather than expose shortcomings to the public, and turned to teaching with great success.

Ralph Guldahl was a curious mixture. He possessed a rugged charm that he never used to advantage. Speech for him was essentially a foreign language, a Pyrrhic victory over silence. Off the course it was as though a piece of seaweed had been removed from its watery element and was stranded. Golf was his element. Out of it he seemed a ghost of himself, but on the fairways he dominated his opponents. We could do with more of his ilk today.

Henry Picard is another long forgotten, but, to those who recall the pre-War giants, his memory lingers. He was quiet-spoken, yet outspoken. His upright and defiant character was mirrored in his face and form. As a golfer he was the ideal model on which to base an uncomplicated style. One of his high-spots came in 1932 when, in a play-off for the Carolina Open, he thrashed the nigh-invincible Walter Hagen by ten strokes. Six years later the New Englander entered the fifth Masters Tournament. Snead was the favourite in an exceptionally strong entry. Harry Cooper set the pace with 68. Snead fell by the wayside with a disastrous 78. The home professional Ed Dudley threatened but faltered after leading the second round. Sarazen blew up. Nelson was no more than consistent. Guldahl tied with Cooper on the 287 mark. Picard was last off among the possible contenders. From that vantage-point he kept tabs on the scores, carded 4 under par for the outward half, and ran out winner by two shots. Over a long playing career, this victory was a peak, on a par with his 1939 win over Byron Nelson at the thirty-seventh hole for the United States PGA title.

Billy Casper, born in San Diego on 24 June 1931, was a frequent and popular visitor to the United Kingdom. He played eight times in the Ryder Cup match, which reflects the consistency of his form, was recognized twice by being nominated Player of the Year, and was three times recipient of the Byron Nelson Award. Apart from innumerable tournament

Horton Smith was the stylist of the Golden Age with fluent rhythm and delicate touch. His talents were many without ever seeming to exhaust his resources.

Henry Picard is long forgotten by many, but to those who recall the pre-War giants his memory lingers like a ghost. He was quiet-spoken, yet out-spoken. His upright and defiant character was mirrored in his face and form. As a golfer he was an ideal model on which to base an uncomplicated style.

successes, Casper won the United States Open Championship in 1959 and 1966, the Canadian Open Championship in 1967, the Italian Open Championship in 1975, and the Masters Tournament in 1970. He retired from competitive golf, then began an Indian Summer of success on the Veterans Circuit with its rejuvenating stake-money bait.

In public Casper sometimes displays a kind of diffidence that conceals and often protects an enormous private egotism. Externally he is emphatically the true professional, as smooth and as hard as perspex. This granite, knowing presence could be something of a screen for behind lurks a shrewd and sensitive man. Few golfers understand more of the game's techniques. It would seem that Billy Casper's natural talents followed his inclinations.

George Archer, born in San Francisco on 1 October 1939, turned professional when he was twenty-five, and persevered, producing good workmanlike results without hitting the headlines until everything came right at Augusta when he won the Masters Tournament in 1969. His physical presence is overwhelming. With brows contracted above tawed jowls, eyes bulging with reproach, and a frame 6 foot 7 inches in height, one feels the soul of the last American bison might easily migrate. In public life Americans are rarely ironic about themselves. Golfers, on the other hand, are frequently self-critical to a radical degree unknown even in this self-deprecatory country. George Archer is one of the severest critics of himself, in many ways unjustifiably. From the onlooker's viewpoint on the sideline it is always exciting to watch a massive professional lashing into the ball with a fury beyond the reach of his weaker and smaller colleagues.

Byron Nelson was one of the few among outstanding contemporaries who, by brilliant example, showed the way along which professional golf should develop. That reputation was not gained without struggles and disappointments. Born 4 February 1912 in Fort Worth, Texas, Nelson turned professional at twenty-one. but made no headway in his home State. He switched to the New York district, made a slight impression, but ran short of funds. On the verge of quitting, he won the Metropolitan Open Championship and collected stake-money of 600 dollars. That success was the turning point. He never looked back. In 1939 Nelson won the United States Open Championship, the Western, North and South, the Vardon Trophy and was runner-up in the PGA Championship. Prior to this he had won two Masters titles. Like Richard Burton in England, the expected advantages of such success were cancelled by the outbreak of war. Even so, Nelson's international reputation was established. He was among the

George Archer has a presence that is overwhelming. It is always exciting to see this massive professional lashing into the ball with a fury beyond the reach of his weaker and smaller colleagues.

Gay Brewer had a fair measure of success in competitive golf but not as much as his skill deserved. The high-spot was winning the Masters Tournament after losing a triple play-off for the title the previous year. I would also add the Ben Hogan Award in 1973.

élite to be judged on their level. Style-wise, his high-hand one-piece swing ran counter to the classic Scottish method and was forerunner of today's methods. In retrospect Byron Nelson is remembered as the professional golfer *par excellence*.

Picking out past Masters winners I think of Gay Brewer, the rugged professional whose perky, crumpled face became a scowling glare when he found trouble. He indulged in a quiet gamesmanship that took the form of a lofty approach to opponents. In the case of Cary Middlecoff, the absence of rigid orthodoxy of style and the degree of his empathy was the yardstick of his stature. He became a great golfer and conflicting elements developed into complements. Twice winner of the United States Open, the roster of success included the Masters title in 1955.

One final name is Jimmy Demaret, born Texas 1910, turned professional 1927, and one of the most delightful personalities to grace the American golfing scene. A warm avuncular man, a jolly man, a genial man, a man without cant or pride, he created an ambience in which ludicrous anomalies grew believable, emitting wisecracks by which he hoped would convince you he was a simpleton. In fact, Demaret was as sharp as a tack. He was a wit as only an American can be witty. With his friend Bing Crosby they made a first-class team, both vocal and golf-wise.

Demaret's record was a graph of his skill. He made three Ryder Cup appearances and figured in the American World Cup winning team of 1961. He won the Argentine Open Championship in 1941 and was leading money winner in 1947, but it was at Augusta that he shone three times. In 1940 he proved that Snead was not the only Texan to win the Masters. The entry attracted the cream of talent, most prominent was Demaret in flamboyant clothes of rainbow hues, and high-heeled Texan boots worn off the course. This happy-go-lucky approach was rewarded with an opening round of 67, later eclipsed by Mangrum's sensational 64. In the end Demaret's consistency won the event by four shots. Then, as sometimes happens, form deserted him. His name no longer appeared in the stake-money table. In 1947 the winning flair returned. He won the Masters by 2 shots from Nelson and Stranahan, gladdening the horizon with an ensemble of canary yellow. In 1950 the performance was repeated, this time two strokes better than Jim Ferrier, acknowledging applause at the prize-giving ceremony by crooning a song into the microphone in the Crosby tradition. Jimmy Demaret was a tonic off and on the fairways.

The 1991 Masters provided possible reasons for the decline of American domination of the golfing scene, a tendency that had become increasingly

Jimmy Demaret was one of the most delightful personalities to grace the American scene. His record was a graph of skill. He made three Ryder Cup appearances, and figured in the American World Cup winning team of 1961. He won the Argentine Open Championship in 1941 and was leading money winner in 1947, but it was at Augusta that he shone three times. In every way Jimmy was a tonic off and on the fairways.

Arnold Palmer invokes the heavens as Ken Venturi putts and Gary Player adds his quota.

evident during the previous ten years. This trend has led to sensitivity about 'foreign' challengers that did not surface during the triumphant Nicklaus era. The ruling at Augusta has always limited the number of non-Americans who could be invited. Even more stringent restrictions now apply to all major American events. This bar is a blunt reminder that foreign entries are not welcome. It has been a double-edged move and not to American advantage long term. Home victories are now virtually assured as tournaments are patronized with entries that other sports might describe as selling-platers. Courses are manicured, greens over-watered to encourage low scoring, inflated sponsorship has boosted stake money. Professionals are no longer as hungry for success as they used to be. There is no need to spend hours on the practice ground. Near luxury style of living is now possible even for those who will never know the winner's rostrum. The needle of fierce competition is less. Even no-hopers can end up with healthy cheques.

European competition is more open, often razor-keen with intense rivalry. Venues are more varied. Greens are not doctored. Rough lives up to its name. Climatic variations call for a wider range of shot-making. Inevitably in such an atmosphere standards of play improve. In the past an invitation to a British professional to play in the Masters was almost an act of charity. The first one to finish in the Top Twenty was Peter Butler, an 'unknown' to American galleries. He slotted thirteenth place in 1964 due to a brilliant third round of 69, then fourteenth in 1966 and twenty-fourth in 1967. At that time Tony Jacklin was knocking on the door, quietly at first with twenty-fourth in 1968, improved to fourteenth in 1970, then later that year shook the Americans rigid by winning the United States Open Championship. The tide had began to turn. Three years later Peter Oosterhuis shared third place with Jack Nicklaus and Bob Goalby. The next year it was Maurice Bembridge's turn. He finished ninth with a total of 283 that included a final round of 68, leaving him five shots adrift from Gary Player's winning aggregate.

The Americans now accepted that on their soil Europeans were not push-over rookies. Severiano Ballesteros confirmed their worst fears at Augusta. Eighteenth in 1978, twelfth in 1979, the Spaniard's tally spoke for itself afterwards. Twice first, second; twice third; fourth, fifth and seventh. The next shock was the claiming of the famous green jacket by Bernhard Langer and Sandy Lyle. It was then Nick Faldo's turn, his purple patch persisted, and finished only four shots short in 1991 of chalking-up a hat-trick of Masters' titles. The winner was diminutive Ian Woosnam,

Elation as Ian Woosnam sinks the winning putt at Augusta. (*Allsport*)

who settled the issue by sinking a seven-footer on the 18th green. America's pride was further jolted through Jose-Maria Olazabel finishing runner-up.

International opinion was reflected at that time in the Sony World Ranking Top Twelve that included seven non-Americans: Ian Woosnam, Jose-Maria Olazabel, Nick Faldo, Greg Norman, Mark McNulty, Bernhard Langer and Severiano Ballesteros. There is no doubt that American successes in the majors have been limited. Mark Calcavecchia was the only American to win the Open Championship over a stretch of seven years. At Augusta he admitted he had not won since that Troon day in 1989. Even the Ryder Cup, for long an American picnic, has not stayed on the other side of the Atlantic for nine years. It was noticeable in the 1991 Masters that the United States challenge was taken up by two veterans, Tom Watson, whose last major win had been in 1987, and Lanny Wadkins, both 41. Up-and-coming home professionals just dropped out of contention.

On the evidence, European and in particular British professionals now lead the world. It may not last. Good times seldom do. Hurt pride could spark an American revival. In the meantime we are riding the crest of the world. Shades of Henry Cotton, the Triumvirate, Harold Hilton and John Ball will doubtless salute this galaxy of talent and the skills that produced such results.

Reassuring Postscript

Statisticians estimate that the average of crime among good golfers is lower than in any class of the community except possibly bishops. Since Willie Park won the first championship at Prestwick in the year 1860, there has, I believe, been no instance of an Open Champion spending a day in prison.

P. G. Wodehouse: *The Clicking of Cuthbert*

INDEX

Page numbers in *italics* refer to illustrations